"What were y

A humorous look at living together under lockdown and its aftermath

by Ray Frith

with

Val Frith

"One of the problems I guess that most people had during this time was what to do about getting their hair cut. This did not always go well..."

Published by New Generation Publishing in 2022

Copyright © Ray Frith 2022

First Edition

The author asserts the moral right under the Copyright, Designs and Patents Act 1988 to be identified as the author of this work.

All Rights reserved. No part of this publication may be reproduced, stored in a retrieval system or transmitted, in any form or by any means without the prior consent of the author, nor be otherwise circulated in any form of binding or cover other than that which it is published and without a similar condition being imposed on the subsequent purchaser.

ISBN: 978-1-80369-692-8

www.newgeneration-publishing.com

New Generation Publishing

Dedicated to Valerie Frith
The world is a sunnier place when she is there

Acknowledgements

Thanks to David Atherton and Charlie Gray who have helped me greatly in getting this book published.

Lockdown *(March 2020)*

Due to our underlying health conditions, and being the age we are, both Val and I have gone into hibernation and have self-isolated.

Day 1 of lockdown, and I'm pleased to report that it has been a success. "Result" I say. "We have not killed each other!"

Day 2 of lockdown, and we discover "daytime television."

"Maybe this will fill the void in the coming weeks" commented Val.

We watch a programme called "Escape to the Country." The plot is that two everyday people look at three houses, choose one and move.

"No" I say. "You surely cannot have just that as a programme, all it would be is watching someone else live a life while you just sit there with yours slipping away. There must be hidden meanings, plot twists and unexpected revelations, so lets stick with it – and I'm certain you'll see."

"Are you sure about that?" asks Val.

"Anyway imagine the conversation when they decided to do this..."

"I would like to move."

"OK – where?"

"To the country – say Devon."

"Fine – lets see... how do we go about this? Estate agents? Tour the area? Survey house prices?"

"Good heavens no! We telephone the BBC at once."

"Of course – why didn't I think of that!"

So in each episode they look at houses, one of which is made deliberately unsuitable. "They've added that to retain interest perhaps?" I wondered.

"So where's the jeopardy?" I ask.

"Ah – I think I have got it - you just won't know which one they will choose until the end of the programme, I think that's meant to have you on the edge of your seat until then" replies Val.

"Er ..right.. slightly disappointed that there's no plot twist though – I think it needs a plot twist."

"There might be. Let's wait and see" says Val.

"They didn't like any of those so they have found a place somewhere else completely" says the commentator.

"There it is! See! Bet you didn't see that coming" says Val.

We sit there for a minute in silence.

"You know I commented yesterday on the fact that we hadn't killed each other" I say. "Can we please? I've changed my mind."

Despite the fact that we could get priority for home delivery from the supermarkets, Val was not sure that they would continue without interruption, so she decided that as we had an as yet unused bread maker and the necessary ingredients to hand, she would give it a try. I didn't realise it at the time but this was to instigate my as yet incomplete transition to master chef. (I'm still working on it.)

The Bread Maker *(April 2020)*

We had been given a bread maker from a friend and it had taken on the appearance of a much-loved ornament, in that we kept looking at it, it never moved, yet kept needing dusting.

"I'm going to make my own bread today" Val announced this morning. In a fit of enthusiasm a few weeks ago she had bought loads of bread making constituents and she had read them out in a list, all of which I can't remember as I had lost the will to live when she told me.

"I'm quite happy with Sainsbury's multi-seed" I commented both hopefully and helpfully.

"That's not helping" she replied, which I guess knocked out the second point. Regarding the first point, I didn't hold out much hope for that either as she followed up with "We're having a Sainsburys delivery this evening but I'm making my own bread."

I was tasked with preparing it on the worktop and sorting out the bits and pieces. "Now we can really get down to it" commented Val with more enthusiasm than I felt necessary.

"What are these for?"

"Those are the kneading blades" I replied with the air of years of knowledge. "You place one large one and one small on to the kneading shaft and rotate them until they click." She was impressed. I didn't think it necessary to tell her that I had just read it out of the instruction manual.

I go through life usually with an air of general puzzlement. For instance, when Eskimos became Inuits, I didn't see the change happen, it had totally passed me by. Coronavirus became Covid-19 and again I missed it – when did that happen? Suddenly "I'm making bread" had become "We're making bread." I had missed that change as well.

My turn to be impressed now. She just chucked everything she had weighed out into the machine, shut the lid and turned it on.

"In three and a half hours we'll have our first loaf, and look at the booklet - it says that '...when you remove your perfect loaf you'll want to show it off to your friends who will invariably waste no time at all in eating it' – I can't wait."

"Only problem with that is..." I pointed out "...nothing is happening." We left it for a while.

Suddenly there was a noise from the kitchen. We rushed in to see the good news that it had started working with the blade rotating in the correct manner. The bad news was that the gloop was turning into what looked like a cross between porridge and wallpaper paste.

"Are you sure it should look like that?" I asked, as I wistfully thought back to the days of Sainsbury's multi-seed, which was only last week but seemed like years ago.

"It's my first time – how should I know? I've followed the recipe to the letter." Val replied, although I felt that her confidence was ebbing away somewhat. To be fair though, as time went by the smell of baking bread was nothing if not encouraging.

So, three hours later, with urgent beeping from the machine, the bread was ready. We examined the contents.

"It's very springy" said Val prodding it.

"I think you could bounce a ball off it as far as I can see" I replied. "Are you sure you can't change the Sainsburys order?"

Time to empty it out. I turned it upside down. Nothing happened. I shook it. Nope. Nothing again. "It's stuck like glue" I said.

"Well, you did call it wallpaper paste" commented Val.

"Not helpful and not funny" I said.

There had been another change and once again I had missed it. "We're making bread had now become "You're making bread."

I had to actually prize the bread out of the tin and it ended up in pieces on the board.

"I know it looks a mess but I'm guessing it'll taste fine" she said, more in hope than expectation.

We tasted it. There followed a long period of silence, whilst both of us waited for the other to speak.

I cracked first. "That is probably the most disgusting thing I have ever tasted in my life."

"Don't hold back, will you" replied Val, "although you do have a point" she added as she walked over to the bin. I don't know what she did there, but I made sure I didn't look.

"Let's analyse what went wrong. The crust has taken on the consistency of a car tyre, the taste is so salty that it surely is a danger to human life, and the inside is just crumbling into nothing." That was my list.

The remains of the first attempt

"Anything to add?" I asked.

"I think that about sums it up" came the reply. "But I have two bits of good news."

"Well?"

"I did order two multi-seed loaves from Sainsburys – just in case!"

"What's the other?"

"I'm going to have another go tomorrow."

We were used to lockdown now and Val was intent on stocking up on groceries "just in case" - of what I didn't know.

Insurrection *(May 2020)*

There are areas in a house where in the natural course of things certain members of the household rule. The kitchen for instance is Val's domain as she makes clear and I am required, in essence, to do what I am told there.

However the garage, I like to think, is my area, where whatever I say goes. We have a modern garage, and therefore, unless we invest in a Sinclair C5 *(Arch.)* there is no way our car will fit into it. Therefore the space is all my own.

"What shall we do with the old freezer?" Val wondered as the shiny new all singing all dancing version had been installed just before lockdown.

"I know, it is still useable, so we could put it in the garage and use it as a spare. We just need to move a few of your things that you have never used and it'll fit in quite nicely. You could get rid of some of it as well at the same time."

I decided not to mention the unused pasta maker that had been in the kitchen cupboard for years taking up space, and instead protested "They are in the garage just in case," but unwillingly moving a box of old CDs (well, isn't streaming the bees knees these days? – or so my sons say), ten years worth of running medals (don't want them, but cannot bring myself to chuck them) and non-working Christmas lights (no explanation for why they are there) anyway.

"You're not hoarding are you?" I added.

We had ordered our groceries on line and there was the first delivery.

"Sorry, but that shelf next to the freezer would be good for the items I can't fit into the cupboard. Can you move your things? After all you rarely use most of it." Val was now well into ordering on line.

I decided not to mention the bread maker, which was still exactly where it was when it first entered the kitchen, and set about moving a gazebo (for which I couldn't find the roof), a box of maps (should have been taken to an auction months ago, but maybe one day I'll look through them) and a box of leads (always left over each time I update the computerware, but look much too important to get rid of).

"Well I think you are hoarding" I said.

"It's a carefully managed strategy for coping if things get tough or I lose the delivery slots" came the firm reply.

"Perhaps we could just organise a couple of shelves so that I can separate the greengrocery from the rest, so can you move the rest of your things there. ...and by the way your side is a mess" she said as the next delivery came in. Sides? I didn't know there were sides. The mess was clearly because I was having to move all this stuff.

I decided not to mention the mandolin, stored in the kitchen, still in its box and unused, as she thought it was too dangerous to use, and duly cleared the shelves of a large number of old picture frames (who would throw away a perfectly good picture frame anyway?), a windbreak which had been there for at least five years (I'm not going to sit on a windy beach, what's the point?) and some old folding chairs (well you never know when twelve people may call at the same time).

"The garage is in a total mess, and it's all your things that's causing it" she announced, "and if you are not going to sort it then I am."

"Hoarder!" I replied. I wish I'd thought of something better.

And that was it.

Due to Coronavirus Val now has control of the garage. As perfect a 'coup d'état' as you will ever see.

...but I am still in charge of the shed.

To pass the time we read the newspapers from cover to cover and I came across an article on road repairs. I am well aware that the following will only be understood by those of a 'certain age.' Sadly, since writing this, Bernard Cribbins passed away at the age of 93 in 2022.

Potholes *(May 2020)*

The Digital Intelligence Brokerage (DIB), no, I didn't know we have one either, has produced a report which, amongst other things, has advised that pothole repairs should be circular, and not square to avoid weak spots at the corners. So reports an article in today's "Times." This is indeed a remarkable discovery and surely well worth the budget of £15m *(yes that is correct)* allocated to it.

The modern road surface was widely introduced in the 1920's and it seems extraordinary that it is only now this type of repair has been established as the correct way forward.

I suspect that this report was produced by Civil Servants who have not been themselves at the sharp end, and that the average road worker could have told the powers above many years ago that this would be the best way to repair the roads.

I produce as evidence Mr. Bernard Cribbins, not a road worker of course, but back in 1962 in his recording "Hole in the Ground" firmly suggested that they should be round and not square, and furthermore, he advised what would happen to those who suggested different.

Mr. Cribbins, now well into his nineties, is still going strong, and I suggest that Transport Secretary Grant Shapps, immediately make arrangements for Mr. Cribbins to be appointed as a consultant for all things roadworks, as he is clearly 60 years ahead of modern day thinking, and would be substantially cheaper than the budget currently allowed for this project.

The severe restrictions on leaving the house were now being eased allowing us to go out for longer walks. Val is not a walker but in order to take advantage of the new freedom she thought she had to make an attempt.

The Trevemper Problem *(June 2020)*

The vagaries of the English language are what makes it so interesting to study and I guess for those learning it is probably quite difficult to master. For instance, take words with double meanings. These are called either homonyms or polysemes depending on whether the different uses of the words are related to each other or not. Today, however I came across a phrase which by my calculation had four meanings.

We were out on a walk around the upper part of the Gannel by Trevemper. Val was carrying a rucksack containing a bottle of water. After crossing the footbridge by the boating lake, we turned left on to the footpath that goes up the hill. Val had gone very quiet. About halfway up I broke the silence.

"Are you alright?"

"I'm fine."

With words of multiple meanings the answer lies in the context, but there was no context in this case. It seemed to me that I had about ten seconds to decipher what that meant. After a quick analysis it came down to one of four meanings

a. I'm very happy, I love going out on walks with you and we see so much of the countryside. Couldn't be better.

b. Why is it always a hill? What is it with you Road Runners? Soon as you see a hill, you have to go up it. All that happens is that you have to come down it again. What's wrong with you anyway?

c.   I'm so absolutely not fine. How could you possibly not see this? Didn't want to come in the first place. Moron!

d.   **** ***!

"Shall I carry your rucksack?" I asked timidly.

"Yeah – OK."

I still don't know which of the four meanings was right.

Still trying to fill the time I started to search the internet for random interesting sites.

Facebook Intelligence Tests *(June 2020)*

I like to think that I am of reasonable intelligence. So, when a chance to measure this with an I.Q. test pops up on Facebook I am really up for it! Apparently it is BMI approved no less.

I fill in the twenty questions, it takes 20 minutes but I do it in 12 - and I think I have done exceptionally well if I do say so myself.

So, I click on "retrieve your results" waiting excitedly for the glowing results to pop up.

I get "Please pay £14.99 to retrieve your results...enter your card details here."

I never saw that coming.

Clearly the big test was "Can you spot the catch before you do the test."

...and sadly, I failed it. I did not pay of course - I might be sillier than I thought I was, but I am not that silly.

As we were in the "highly vulnerable" category we still did not go out a great deal and remained on the cautious side. My interest in cookery as a home hobby was beginning to grow.

Man vs. Cream *(July 2020)*

We sat looking at two litres of cream a friend had bought round thinking we might like it. Social distancing meant that she had left it on the doorstep.

"Why have you got that?" I said. It seemed an awful lot of cream for two people.

"Apparently it was on the shelf, the sell-by date was today, they were selling it for £1 and she thought we could make use of it" said Val.

This would seem to be an ideal time to start my cooking career, so I announced "I know what I am going to do – I'm going to make butter."

I remember as a kid my mother would allow us to beat the cream but with a stark warning – if you beat it too much it'll turn into butter. As a 10-year-old I did not believe that for one minute. I now had the chance to see if I was right or wrong.

"Does that actually involve any cooking at all?" mused Val to herself, but loud enough to let me hear.

"One bowl and a ton of cream – and away we go" I thought ignoring all her doubts. I had the beater on at full pelt and immediately sprayed the wall, the counter, the floor, myself but not Val who had seen it coming.

"Reckon I'll slow that down a bit on reflection" I muttered while Val got busy with a cloth. This was all under the gaze of someone who really had no faith in my ability with this task. But I was intrepid and eventually... success – the liquid turned solid and split.

"Ah... I think I have forgotten a jug to tip the buttermilk into" I said hoping that Val, who was now mopping the floor, would be impressed that I knew it was buttermilk.

She provided a jug but was not impressed at all as it was a wide bowl and a narrow jug, with the result that it spilt when I transferred it and she switched her efforts from the floor to the counter, now running with liquid. I then had to squeeze the bits of butter and wash them.

"I'm sorry to ask again" I said as she finished wiping up. "Would you mind getting me another bowl as I have to put the squeezed butter into it." I distinctly heard grumbling. However, I finished this part of the process and was ready to go.

By now Val had started on the walls. "Whilst you are there can I have a few pots to put the butter in?" I did ask very nicely.

"Look I am not your sous chef – why didn't you get this all out at the start?" she said. I thought this was a somewhat severe reply, but to be honest I could see where she was coming from.

All done, and the butter looked just the part in its pots. The kitchen on the other hand, did not.

The Homemade Butter

"I've made butter! I'm going to call it 'I can't believe it is butter'" I proudly exclaimed "...and all on my own!" Probably a mistake to say that given her reaction, but what has been said cannot be unsaid.

She picked up the salt. "...and how much salt did you put in?" She asked.

"It'll be slightly salted" I said authoritatively. This was a lie of course as I had completely forgotten it.

Ah well!

One of the problems I guess that most people had during this time was what to do about getting their hair cut. This did not always go well...

The Haircut *(July 2020)*

"Time for another haircut I think" I mused looking critically in the mirror. Lockdown meant of course that it had to be done at home.

No sooner said than Val had the bathroom mirror on the kitchen table and had scissors in hand. She seemed more enthusiastic than I thought necessary, especially as last time after a trim I was unable to find hardly any trace of hair on the floor.

"I'm going to go for it this time" she said.

After a few minutes of snipping, I studied the result. This is where I could have bitten my tongue off for saying it, and again, once said of course, it cannot be unsaid.

"It's actually growing faster than you are cutting it" was my comment.

This did not go down well.

"Right!" came the response.

Ice formed on the walls as she changed from timidity to – and I use the word after careful thought - temerity.

The comb started to catch my ears each time she used it and when she brushed the cut hair off, did I imagine it or did I receive an 'accidental' cuff around the head? ...and what was she doing round the back where I couldn't see it in the mirror?

There was about five minutes of watching hair cascade downwards.

"There – done!" Val was looking triumphant. "You said you wanted a haircut and now you have one."

I tried to work out what her tone indicated. My hair was certainly shorter at the front, but I still didn't know what the back of my head looked like and there was a great deal of hair on the floor. It was all very suspicious.
However, has Val really thought this through? It won't be long before she too will need a haircut.

...and I will be ready and waiting!

It was quite clear that a number of small businesses were suffering due to the lockdown and Val felt that it was right for us to support them wherever possible. Locally of course the fishing industry was suffering badly, not only because of Covid but from Brexit as well.

The Lobster Part I *(July 2020)*

"We must do something" said Val.

"What's that?"

"We have to help the fishermen – they have caught all that fish and their market has almost totally disappeared. I've seen that we can join the "Newquay Buy Sell & Swap" Facebook page and we can buy fish direct from the quay. Can you join us up?"

"OK, I've done that – what now?"

"It's shellfish that are usually sent abroad, so I want to buy a lobster! It'll help them and we can live it up a little."

"You have to be kidding me – they are about £20 at the shops and by the way, someone has to shell it."

"I thought you could – this guy is offering one for £10."

"Well ..er.. I suppose I could do that, I've shelled a crab before – how different can it be?"

"Fine" said Val.

Hmm... in my opinion that was said too quickly. There is something not quite right here. By this time though, Val was on the telephone.

"Yes... just one lobster, caught same day, and we'll be down at the harbour at 5 o'clock to pick it up."

"That was quick" I said. "Should we not have thought about this a bit?" I still felt that all was not right.

"No, it's all fine. We'll have it for dinner tonight. I'll do all the trimmings, we can open a sparkly, and you can kill the lobster, shell it and cook it"

"Hang on there – did you say kill it?"

"Oh... yes" she said innocently. "Did I not mention that? If you buy a lobster direct from a boat it has to be sold alive – apparently it's the law."

"No, you didn't mention that – I think I might have remembered."

"Let's look up how to do it on Google – there – you see...

...OMG that's not how it's done is it?" she gasped.

This is how we came to be having egg and chips tonight. One lobster's life saved.

The Lobster Part II *(August 2020)*

We were in St. Agnes. Val was still intent on helping the fishermen during the crisis by buying direct from them and had heard that there was one on the Chapel Porth road selling from his garage.

I waited in the car at a suitable socially acceptable distance and watched as she came out laden with bags looking somewhat triumphant.

"I've got hake, sea bass, crab, scallops and..." She paused for dramatic effect.

"...this!" and pulled out from the bag a very large and very red lobster.

"Hell's teeth, not again" I blurted out. "I so hope it's dead this time."

"As a doornail" said Val, stuffing it back in the bag. I debated whether to discuss with her the merits of this expression first noted in the 13th century and also used by Dickens in 'A Christmas Carol', but decided instead to discuss who was going to cook it.

"You are" came the reply, which I kind of knew anyway.

Back in the kitchen, the first task of course was to shell it. Turned it over, ran a knife down the length and back and it butterflied quite easily, except for the shell which was annoyingly springy and folded it back up as soon as it was back on the board. What you should not do, as I found out, is to pick it up and bend it backwards, as although flexible, it suddenly snaps and showers you (i.e., me) with some very oozy brown meat. I looked up. Val was standing at the kitchen door, saying nothing, with a totally blank expression but I just had this feeling that inside she was laughing like a drain.

"So is that all we have got?" she asked looking at a very small bowl holding the meat content and the very large bowl containing round about four fifths of what we had bought. "At that price you're going to have to do something with the shell – tell you what, make a soup."

"I'll be making a bisque" I replied in as a superior manner as I could muster.

I needed to smash the contents of the bowl into small pieces, so I used a rolling pin, draped kitchen roll over the top to stop pieces flying upwards and started to whack.

On reflection that was not well thought through. To be fair nothing flew upwards. All sorts of gunge, general detritus and shell just flew sideways across the kitchen instead. I looked up to see Val back at the door with the same blank expression.

"How's the soup going?" she enquired innocently.

"Look – it's a bisque" I said slightly impatiently and took five to clear up the mess.

Who knew that a bisque would need celery and carrot and also sherry, none of which we had got. Val was dispatched to the local shop to rectify but refusing to buy the sherry. "We don't drink it, no-one who is likely to visit will drink it and I'm not spending £15 on a bottle just to put in a dash in your soup."

"Bisque" I corrected her silently.

Now I know that bay leaves are not crisp. Well, these ones were. I looked at the sell-by date – March 2016! This did not faze Val.

"Oh, just put a few extra in" she advised.

"Yes, but...2016? What other antiquities have you got stored in there?" I queried. One of her looks shut me up on that one.

An hour and a half later it was blending time. To be honest, this did not go too well either. There was too much mixture for the blender really and it went over the maximum line by about half an inch. I decided that I would take a chance, and making sure that I kept my hand on the lid firmly, the seal should hold and all would be OK. All that happened was that liquid shot out of every join and covered my hand, the liquidiser and the work surface.

"Guess that was not as good a seal as I thought it would be" I muttered and looking round saw Val, once again at the door with the same blank expression.

"There are some instructions for using that in the cupboard, if it helps" she said, again innocently, but decidedly not helpfully.

Finally, all done, and the mixture was in packs ready for storage.

"A really good-looking soup" was her verdict.

"Look – you keep calling it a soup – it's a bisque, don't you know the difference?" I was getting just a bit tetchy.

"About £15 as far as I can see" came the reply. She had been doing the maths. "...and I do know the difference" she added. "I just like winding you up."

We had a taster, and to be fair, Val thought it delicious. "I think that was really worth the effort" she continued after due consideration.

"However, perhaps one small point. I think it just needs a dash of sherry."

The restrictions severely impacted on our ability to celebrate family events properly. There were some things we could still do though and exchanging cards was one of them.

Our First Date – 33 Years On *(August 2020)*

"I'm increasingly worried about the future of the planet" announced Val.

Not something I was expecting to hear first thing on a Monday morning, and especially not on our first date anniversary. I decided to go with it though.

"Is there anything in particular which has bought this about?" I enquired, trying to look more enthusiastic than I actually was. I should point out that of course I was enthusiastic about it, but it's just at 8.30 on a Monday morning I was more interested in the future of my croissant which was rapidly getting cold.

"It's global warming" she continued. "The world should not be cutting down trees just to produce paper. The world should be much more frugal about such things. It's all to do with CO2."

"I should say so" I agreed, at the same time pondering whether I should just go for it and start eating, or whether it would show an inordinate lack of interest in the world climate emergency. "But how can the UK on its own affect things?"

"Well, we could plant more trees, but the available land is limited, so the UK could, as an alternative, consume less paper."

By now I reckoned that it was stone cold, and my cup of tea was going the same way, but of course the planet had to come first.

"Well in that case, each household in the UK should play its part."

I tried to be as emphatic as possible.

"We ourselves should use less paper. We'll make it our axiom" I announced. Surely brownie points should be oozing from every pore! I had sacrificed my breakfast to the fight against global warming.

"I've made a start by recycling" she replied, and produced a card. I opened it and could not help but notice it was the 30th anniversary card from three years ago. The 30 had been crossed out and replaced with 33.

"Happy anniversary!"

Suddenly it all became clear. "You forgot to get a card didn't you" I ventured.

At that point I decided that I would heat up my croissant and my tea in the microwave which I did not think would impact the planet greatly, because the carbon footprint would be offset by the recycled card.

"Oh alright... yes I did" came the rather subdued reply, but I suddenly realised too late that I was heading for dangerously choppy waters.

"By the way, where's my card?" she added enquiringly but actually clearly knowing the answer.

If I had been quick enough I would have responded with "No card of course – I was thinking of the planet."

In the event I sank without trace.

27

By now we were well used to being together for a majority of the time but on the odd occasion some conversations could be misinterpreted.

Punctuation *(August 2020)*

I have, in the past, been a little punctilious about the standard of punctuation in text. For instance, I have on some occasions had to rant about the misuse of (or missing) apostrophes. However, at the moment I am looking into the use of question marks, are they necessary?

An example – today I emptied all the bins in the house into a black sack and left it in a corner of the kitchen. My concern surrounds this sentence quoted verbatim from Val:

"Are you going to put that outside."

Is it right to put a question mark or a full stop after this?

The modern thinking I suppose is that with the onset of texting and the like, you need not bother and I am sure that many of the younger generation don't.

However I am a traditionalist and would suggest that every question should end with a question mark, as indeed would normally be the case here. But after some consideration I have not done this.

The observant will know why of course.

It was not a question.

I felt that my cooking ability was really ramping up now, so I was ready for any task that Val was likely to throw at me.

The Sous Chef *(September 2020)*

"I need some help for dinner tonight," said Val.

"What do you need?"

"I'm thinking you could make a cauliflower puree."

"I'm on it."

Now, that was easy to say, but I certainly could not even guess the ingredients, and apart from cauliflower, I hadn't a clue what went into it. Google to the rescue, and with my previous encounter with cream safely forgotten, I was ready, and as the saying goes, what could possibly go wrong?

"Why are you crawling round the kitchen floor?" Val had seen me from the lounge through the glass door.

"I had hoped you hadn't seen me" I replied. "Funny story actually, and not my fault. There was a pot of coleslaw in the 'fridge with clingfilm on but slightly loose. The cream had a sticky label off at the edge and the clingfilm had stuck to it, so as I pulled out the cream, the coleslaw came with it. I'm just cleaning up the floor."

"But - can I point out that you put the clingfilm on it, so in a sense I suppose one could say that it was your fault?" I said. The look was enough for me to backtrack on that one sharpish.

The recipe called for copious amounts of cream, so once the onions had been cooked until soft in butter, I added the double cream. Almost a pot later it went through my mind that it

seemed very thick, and come to think of it, a slightly funny colour.
"I hope it's not off" I thought and went to the pot to check the sell-by date.

I jumped a mile. "OMG it's custard!"

Now I make the point that looking at the pictures on the carton, the main thing that stuck out were the words "Double Cream" which was part of the contents rather than "Custard" which in my opinion should have been the larger print, and all I had done was glance at it when I took it out of the 'fridge. Surely an easy mistake to make, was my take on it.

The offending pot – it clearly has "Double Cream" in the largest print.

I rest my case!

Do women have a sixth sense about these things? Val was at the door. "OK what have you done now?"

"Another funny story actually..." and after explaining, I had achieved a first – I made Val totally speechless. She disappeared, shaking her head and I started again.

All fine this time and the complete concoction was left simmering on the stove until the cauliflower was soft.

"What's that noise, and what's that smell? Val wondered out loud.

I dived for the kitchen, unfortunately not quite in time to stop the mixture bubbling over the saucepan on to the hot plate. I was desperately trying to clean it off before it triggered the fire alarm.

"Surely you know not to put a lid fully on a saucepan full of milk and cream" she said, in what was I thought, a rather marked tone.

"It's only supposed to be simmering" I explained.

"So why have you got the hotplate on 4?" She queried.

"Oh, so I have - silly me" I replied, trying to make a lighthearted joke of it. "Just forgot to turn it down, thats all."

We had cauliflower puree with our meal and it tasted fine as Val had to admit, and looked good too.

"What's for afters" I queried.

"Well, it's not going to be custard is it" said Val, grimly.

Funny the things you do when you are confined to the house for an extended period. For Val, one of these was to audit the sell by dates on the herbs and spices.

Herbs and Spices *(October 2020)*

"You remember when you were making your lobster soup, you commented on the bay leaves being antiquities, and were there any further antiquities in the cupboard?" said Val yesterday, deliberately forgetting that it was a bisque that I had made. "Well, I took it to heart and today I am going to audit my spice and herb cupboard."

"Now, there is something else I want you to do" she continued.

"What's that?"

"Oh, I had nothing in mind, just something else" came the reply.

She clearly did not want me around – and of course, all the more reason to stay. Apart from getting the crisp bay leaves, I had not ventured into the depths of that part of the kitchen cupboards.

"I bet there is a myriad of different herbs used once and then forgotten" I pondered. "For instance, I remember we used to use ground black pepper, but for a long time now we have ground it out in a pepper mill. I'm sure there was some left."

"Gone a long time ago probably, I wouldn't leave something there like that" said Val as she proceeded to empty out the spice cupboard. "Are you sure there is nothing you could be getting on with?"

"No – I'm fine" I was enjoying this. By now she was emptying the herb cupboard as well. To be quite frank I didn't know there

were even that many herbs and spices in existence at all. "You could open an Indian restaurant with this lot" I surmised.
"Oh – you still here?" was all I got in return.

"Cloves! - look. 2015. They've got to go." I put them in the discarding pile.

"You do know that they don't go off, they just lose flavour over time so all you do is put more in to compensate" she said in a manner meant to show she knew about such things.

I sniffed them. "Actually, I think you could tip the lot in and still not get any flavour at all – and anyway you don't even like the smell of cloves."

"I bought them just in case" came the response. I tried to picture in case of what – but nothing sprang to mind.

"Did you find the pepper amongst that lot?"

"No! - and by the way the car needs petrol, you could go now if you like."

"No chance. I want to see if I can beat 2015" I replied looking at chilli flakes. "Ha! 2013 – I mean 2013, come on!"

The Out-of-Date Contents

Now I know when to carry on, and I know when to retreat. I got the look. "Right, I think it's time I sorted out the garage" I said as I could not see this ending well. I went on my way and left Val to it.

Twenty minutes later I returned to see that a group had been arranged on the side ready for disposal. I had come in unexpectedly and she backed off with a guilty look.

"All these to go" she announced triumphantly. I looked at the unopened packet on the left. It was star anise. Use by date 2011.

"That has to be the eldest - yes?" I asked.

"Bet you don't know what that's for" she said ignoring my comment. She was right, I didn't know. On the other hand, not having opened it since bought in 2011 – did it matter?

"Sorry – but what's that behind your back?" I queried.

"Oh, nothing much." Val was now looking decidedly shifty. She reluctantly produced the missing pot of ground black pepper.

"I knew it" I said. "I knew there was some left."

What's the use by date?"

"2006." There was silence.

"Hang on a minute – where are you going?"

"Just going to check in The Guinness Book of Records."

Probably I will be regarded as a Philistine, but I have never really understood the Turner Prize. I've always regarded the main criteria for art being something that I have not got anywhere near enough talent to produce. I take a "The King's New Clothes" attitude towards the prize and one day a real art expert will be brave enough just turn round and say, "It's not art" and suddenly everyone will realise that they've been duped.

The Turner Prize *(October 2020)*

I was engrossed in the computer as Val passed.

She stopped. "What are you up to?" she asked, probably not expecting an answer but enthusiasm was getting the better of me and I wanted someone to tell.

"I'm researching the Turner Prize" I replied. "It seems to me that if an unmade bed with the witty title 'My Bed' can be a finalist, a suit with a brick pattern on it can win, or even an entry of a group of people standing still for an hour can win it as well, then I have to be in with a chance."

I continued. "There's £25,000 up for grabs – seems to me to be a piece of cake."

"Well what's your proposed exhibit?" said Val, seeming to me to be displaying considerably less enthusiasm than I was.

"Look at this." I produced a picture. "I just need to refine my interpretation, give it a pithy title and we're home and dry. Totally abstract and more than a hint of Jackson Pollock, wouldn't you say? ...and all my own work."

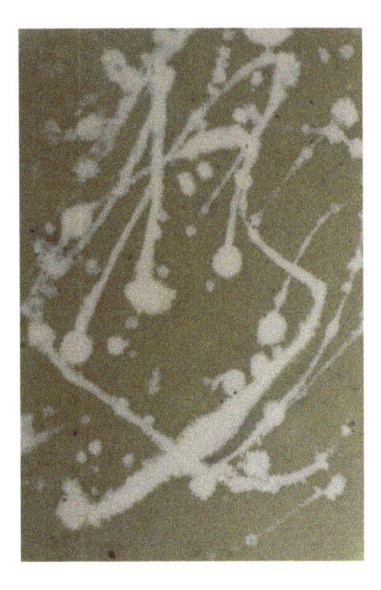

The Proposed Exhibit

Val was less than impressed. "One of our grand-children could have done that" was all I got in return. "Why not just hang it in the garage if you like it so much?"

"Harsh!" I thought, seeing as it was our passport to riches, and she continued – "It does seem familiar though."

"Also, if it had a deformed head in one corner you could say that it was hint of Pablo Picasso or put in a transparent unicorn hanging in the air you could say that it was a hint of Salvador Dali, just add a soup can and it would be a hint of Andy Warhol, and...."

"I think you can stop now" I interrupted. "I get the picture – you just don't appreciate what I'm trying to convey here."

"Well, what is the message?" She asked.

"This is about life - The colour is monotone, muted, and has a subdued pastel quality which is really saying that in general our journey through our existence is generally colourless and muddled. The change of direction of some of the lines shows that our path is not clear and will take unexpected turns at times. The times of note along our journey are clearly represented by the larger spots but their definition is not sharp, telling us that these times can appear without defined boundaries adding to the general maelstrom. Generally speaking, this picture is urging us to consider the hopelessness of our attempt to negotiate our way through the passage of life."

"Don't know why, but I'm sure I recognise it."

"I'm now getting to grips with the title – I'm thinking "Existence is Futile."

"That's the best you can come up with? I though you said you needed a pithy title." She was about to continue when she stopped short.

"I know what this is" she said triumphantly.

"You've taken a picture of the soup you had for lunch! I thought I recognised it. Hang on a minute... it was me who put the cream in. In that case it wasn't all your own work, that's my design and you are a plagiarist."

Rumbled!

I thought quickly. "I know that, and you know that, but this is the Turner Prize, and they won't know that."

Suddenly she was in. "Forget the interpretation and the title..."

She paused.

"...if 'My Bed' does it for them then let's just call it 'My Lunch' and we must be in with a shot."

It might have been my imagination, but it seemed that the number of sales calls we received on the telephone greatly increased during the lockdown period. This was even with us registered with the Telephone Preference Service.

Sales Calls *(November 2020)*

I answered the telephone.
"Hello – How are you?" came an extremely friendly voice on the other end of the line, although with a marked foreign accent.

Immediately I was in a quandary. Clearly a sales call, as they always start with that, but how to answer?

I obviously did not know him from Adam, so why would he be asking after my health? Kind of intrusive I immediately thought. So how to deal with this. It seemed I had a couple of seconds to consider the alternatives...

I thought try "I'm very well thank you." The mistake made would be to stop there. The initiative would be immediately passed across to the caller. He would follow up with "Did you know that you can have your old boiler replaced at no cost to you. How old is your boiler?"

What about "I'm very well thank you – how are you?" Still wrong as he will ignore the reply and still commence with "Did you know that you can have your old boiler replaced..."

Then "I'm very well thank you – how are you?"

"Did you know..."

Interrupt here with "No...seriously - how are you?" Notice here how the initiative would be passed back to me, but I would need to take care...

"I'm well thank you, did you know that you can have your old boiler replaced..." and the initiative has now been immediately switched back again.

Maybe it would be better to try another line of reply.

So "Actually, thank you for asking, I'm not so well at the moment." Again, not good.

"I'm sorry to hear that, but I can perhaps cheer you up because... did you know that you can have your old boiler replaced..."

Perhaps try "That's very caring of you. I am very poorly at the moment. I have a hiatus hernia; my wife has left me and only yesterday my cat died."

Sorry but this would not phase an intrepid salesperson. "Oh dear, I'm so sorry, life can be so cruel, but at least I can hopefully cheer up your day a little. Did you know that you can have your old boiler replaced..."

I settled for "Hi! Great that you telephoned. I so want to tell you the good news. Did you know Jesus said that all sinners can be saved..."

That's as far as I got.

He hung up.

Much home viewing was inevitable during 2020 and I guess the TV was hardly ever off. Well, that was the case in our house.

Box Sets *(November 2020)*

Come on, who on earth would binge watch a box set?

To sit there, in a cosy armchair with copious amounts of drink, alcoholic of course, with unhealthy amounts of food, in a semi-darkened room, shutting out the world, probably most of the relatives as well, and watch the same thing over and over again, with those evil geniuses like Netflix keeping the viewer enslaved by putting a little box in the corner of the screen telling the victim that the next episode starts in ten seconds, is about as meaningless an existence as can be lived. A sad reflection on life today.

We have just discovered on Netflix (OK I admit it – I subscribe) a series called "Designated Survivor." This insidious US import has quietly slithered out of the television without us noticing. We watched an episode from time to time and I thought I was strong enough to resist, but it's already too late. It was time for bed last night, but that little box showed that the next instalment was about to start. We had to watch it.

I now realise that its tentacles have enveloped me, trapping me on my sofa, and will not let me stop watching it. I have watched in horror as Val now too has been caught in its grip.

We now sit there taking in episode after episode. I have caught myself drinking a can of cider whilst watching yesterday, that's the slippery slope in action and sure enough, at the end of each episode once again that little box in the corner shows that there is only ten seconds until the next helping. We are now part of that world.

I've just checked on Google and there are 53 episodes - I mean, 53 episodes. There is no escape. I think we are doomed!

We watched a number of programmes on foraging, an ideal pastime for social distancing, but to be honest I did not retain enough from them to be confident of what I was doing if I went out. However, there was something I could collect that I really could not get wrong, and it would add greatly to my cookery expertise.

Foraging *(December 2020)*

"I've just watched a programme on foraging, and I've decided to give it a go" I announced yesterday to no-one in particular but as Val was the only one there, she took heed by raising an eyebrow.

"Anything in mind?" she queried, and displayed, in my opinion, very little interest.

"Well, what do we have more of, than anything else, in this part of the world?"

"I'm sure you are going to tell me" she correctly surmised.

"Ocean!" I said, like it was a startling revelation. We must make full use of it and that's what I'm going to do."

"I think they call it fishing." I wasn't sure whether she was being ironic or not.

"No, not that. I'm going to produce salt."

"Salt?"

"Yes, salt!

We have an ocean full of it here and I can't see that there will be any problem in producing as much as we want. Pure foraging in my opinion." Val looked doubtful, but there was no stopping me now.

Filling the bottle but not the wellies

Half a dozen bottles in hand we were down in the bay in minutes. There was a bit of a problem that I hadn't considered. The bottles were quite large, and to fill them properly I had to wade out in the wellies further than I would have liked to get the depth. It turned out to be higher than the wellies so I had to do it a little bit at a time between waves which were annoyingly large. Val was bottle holder, and I just had this feeling that she was waiting for my boots to fill with water as she kept the camera at the ready just in case.

For once, things went my way and we got back to the car with bottles of seawater and me with dry feet, but disappointing Val.

"Right, obviously I have got to reduce this down. Around 3.5% of seawater is salt" I announced hoping to impress, "...and I've got to evaporate it down to that figure."

I got the impression however, that she was very much not impressed.
"Look at this." She pulled out of the cupboard a packet of 'Saxa' salt. "£1, I think you'll find, and for 750 grams as well." I had this feeling that things now were beginning to go awry.

"Ah!" I said. "Ah! Mine is pure sea salt – it doesn't compare." Round one to me, I thought.

"What about the fact that Sainsbury's are selling 350 grams of coarse sea salt for 95p?...and as it happens here is a pot."

"Yeah...well I bet it isn't Atlantic Ocean salt" was my less than adequate answer. Definitely round two to her, but worse was to come.

"...and here is my pot of Cornish Sea Salt – 225 grams and £1.70."

The Salt Store

Why anyone would want so much salt is beyond me, but even I thought "game, set and match" though of course I didn't say it. I am nothing if not intrepid, and I was determined to get my salt made despite these setbacks. I put two litres of the seawater in a large saucepan on the stove, and the rest in a number of receptacles on the radiator, sat back and waited.

...and waited and waited.

After a few hours on the radiator nothing had happened to the water levels there at all. Val took a look.

"You know what I am thinking?" She murmured.

"I'm thinking cholera."

"Not a chance" I replied. It's fresh out of the Atlantic. "Remember your geography. The North Atlantic Drift means that there was no pollution for thousands of miles. Anyway wouldn't the salt kill it?"

"...typhoid, hepatitis..."

"OK you can stop now, – the warm water will be there for days at this rate with very little happening, so I see your point. Fair enough, this part of the operation is cancelled."
"...botulism, e-coli, salmonellosis." She was on a roll, but at that point ran out of illnesses.

On the stove, I boiled the water in deference to Val's concerns and then let it simmer to reduce. This was at around 2.30pm. At around 8 o'clock Val came in from the kitchen. "It's like the Eden Project in there. I've just locked the outside door and the key was soaking wet. The water must be going somewhere, and as the evening cools down the condensation will be everywhere."

I looked at the saucepan. There was about an inch of water left. "Look once it goes past the 4% mark it will have to crystallise – it's chemistry, no, scratch that, it's physics, anyway it has to!" I was a lot less certain than I made out.

"You've turned the kitchen into a sauna, goodness knows how much electricity you've used, and even now if we get any salt out of this it will only be a few grams and will have cost a fortune." Val's enthusiasm had run out and reality was beginning to take hold.
Reality also meant that at the same time I didn't know where two litres of water had gone – but gone it had, because at around 11 o'clock like magic the crystals appeared.

100g of sea salt
"We have salt" I shouted. I needed to because Val had gone to bed, after struggling to wait up to see my, and yes, I will use the word, success!

"Look – salt!" I had to show her. She opened an eye and said "that's nice dear" and went back to sleep.

I sat, salt in hand, on my own, very self-satisfied and pondered as to whether it would be possible to turn it into a business. 'Holywell Bay Sea Salt' had a certain ring about it to be sure, but in the event I realised of course that it was never going to happen and toddled off to bed.

However, I made a mental note to have chips for dinner tomorrow.

After all, we have enough salt.

This was to be a Christmas like no other. The Government had introduced a tier system to control Covid. We thought we were in tier three where we lived.

It's Christmas! *(December 2020)*

Well, it's December, and at last the sensible amongst us can start to anticipate the forthcoming Christmas festivities. One of the pleasures of early December is the Advent Calendar.

Ah Yes - this little daily treat just makes the day that bit brighter. A sweet? perhaps a chocolate? may be an uplifting little quote to help one along the way?

No names of course Valerie Frith, but what, in the name of all that is dear, makes anybody put up an Advent Calendar with a daily DIY job in it? ...and what makes them think that any will be opened after seeing the first one?

One of my personal Christmas traditions is to get to Christmas Day without hearing Slade's 'Merry Xmas Everybody' as I have gradually come to find it really annoying over the years, having been around sadly when it first came out.

Suffice to say, and not unexpectedly, I have never been close to making it. This year however, was going to be different. I did everything I could to be away from anywhere that might play it - Morrisons, Radio 2, Val's playlist, certain restaurants etc.

...only to have it snatched away from me, when in one of my most trusted places! I was happily listening to The Archers on Radio 4 this evening feeling quite safe and..nooo! - it was background music to one of the scenes.
I realise now - there is no escape from this wretched song! Not even on Radio 4.

Love 'em or hate 'em, Brussels sprouts are an essential element of Christmas – I was hoping that as were were to be on our own this time these evil evolutions of nature's twisted sagacity would not appear on our table.

Brussels Sprouts *(December 2020)*

The recent problems with Coronavirus and the difficulties of arranging a proper family Christmas has led me to think back over the many years since I was a child, and the memories I have of Christmas dinners of those days.

My parents always had an ultra-traditional Christmas dinner with all the proper trimmings. I, my brother and three sisters would of course attack this with total commitment until of course it came to the Brussels sprouts.

Certainly on my plate, and maybe on my brother and sisters plates, although I don't remember their attitude towards them well, they were left on the side. At this point we would be ordered to eat them, even though at that age I considered them the devil's abomination. We didn't have them at other times of the year, so why now?

My mother would announce grandly in reply "Because it's Christmas."

I was clearly unworldly at that time, but even then the logic of this statement totally escaped me.

Moving forward about sixty years to last week and Val had obtained a delivery slot for the Christmas dinner groceries. I couldn't help but notice that along with the usual items, she had ordered "Brussels sprouts with Pancetta and Chestnuts."

I was guessing that the pancetta and chestnuts were there to mask the totally offensive flavour of the sprouts.

When I queried why she had ordered this (never a wise thing to do) I simply received the reply "Because it's Christmas."

After all these years I still do not understand that logic, but in addition now I'm also wondering why Val has turned into my mother.

Well today the supermarket van turned up, and the Christmas food has been safely delivered.

All bar two items which were out of stock. I looked at the invoice – and with one of the items it said...

"Could not be delivered: Brussels Sprouts with Pancetta and Chestnuts."

I'm going to have a very happy Christmas!

Although I was now evangelistic in my one man attempt to rid the world of these infernal vegetables, I knew it couldn't actually happen. So I had another idea...

On Behalf of Children at Christmas – Part 1
(December 2020)

Thinking about the treatment of children throughout the ages, it does seem that they have had a raw deal. In Victorian times if they were poor they were sent out to work at a very early age in jobs even adults would refuse to do today. If they were rich they would be under the rule of strict disciplinarian nannies acting as substitute parents.

It was still rife the 50s and 60s. I put forward as an example my parents insistence that we should sit at the dinner table until we had eaten our meals in full no matter what we were served or how long it took, and as I have intimated before in these essays, it included at Christmas...Brussels sprouts. The devil's abomination.

Children still suffer from having to eat Brussels sprouts "because it's Christmas" being the illogical reason justifying this cruelty. Well I have discovered what I think is the perfect recipe in order to help the children still in the clutches of these food monsters (parents).

Brussels sprouts with hazelnut mayo! I look at it this way. I reckon if you put enough mayonnaise (does almost every word over four letters have to be abbreviated these days?) on the sprouts you might not be able to taste them at all. The young could swamp their plates with this concoction and just pretend they were enjoying the sprouts without actually having to taste them. How's that children!

Time to consult the oracle. Val, like me is of a certain age and therefore now has a completely balanced view on life, and will consider both the pros and cons of my various suggestions in the field of cookery and give a balanced reply. So eagerly I put to her my suggestion of toned down Brussels, so to speak. She stood silently for a few moments, considering how to reply.

"Are you out of your mind? How could you possibly think that mayonnaise goes with sprouts. It'll be absolutely disgusting. Where on earth did you find a recipe like that?" Well, if that was a balanced view...

I will admit here that my confidence did take a little bit of a knock.

"It was in Saturday's paper. It had Christmas recipes from a number of celebrity chefs. Look – there's Marcus Wareing, Thomasina Myers, Paul Ainsworth..."

Val stopped me in my tracks.

"OK which one produced this?"

"It wasn't one of the famous chefs and the name didn't ring a bell" I replied.

"I see. The one you don't know. Maybe that should tell you something?"

"It was one of those cookery competition winners." I had gone all authoritative. I just looked the name up on Google.

"Well I bet it wasn't won with this on the menu."

"Right" I said. "Christmas is coming and I'm going in to bat for the chef and the children. I don't think they realise that there is a pot of gold here. I'm going to make it on a test basis and then I'll go back to the chef and offer to lead a marketing campaign

on the premise that it is a dish of sprouts for children who don't like sprouts. As obviously it will be a real winner, between us we'll make a killing."
OK, well I've gone over the top here, I'm not going to do that of course, but one can dream!

"I predict disaster, but I'll reserve final judgement until I've tasted it." replied Val. That seemed harsh but fair.

"Actually I wish I'd kept my mouth shut." I thought on reflection.

The list of ingredients included pasteurised egg yoke, hazelnut paste and rice vinegar.

"I'm having a problem with pasteurised egg yolk. You can't buy it and pasteurising it yourself involves fourteen stages." I was at a bit of a loss.

"Oh for goodness sake what are you going on about? Anyone who makes mayonnaise just uses an egg yolk. It's all nonsense." Val seemed most emphatic.

"Well it says that it is essential, especially if you are vulnerable, and as a consequence it could be that you contract salmonella, and for someone of my age that could be fatal." I was unsure.

"Trust me there is no problem" replied Val. It's just a warning to cover themselves - you know like they put that notice on Christmas trees saying you shouldn't eat them. It's rubbish."

"Fair enough." She had managed to convince me to use plain egg yokes and not to worry at all, as everything would be OK and there was no danger of death. We laughed heartily about it, in the same way that we laughed when I took out the Over 50s Life Policy recently, with the guaranteed pay out on my demise. Hmm...

Next job was to visit the supermarket. Val insisted on coming with me, which always raises the stress levels. As usual I parked at the back of the car park ensuring that there were no cars either side, and the usual frank exchange of views followed as to the worth of my parking philosophy. It saves the car side being bashed and it's only a few extra steps, was my argument.

I needed hazelnut paste, and recipe said that I could use Nutella as a substitute. However, every pot on the shelves contained cocoa, chocolate or some other flavour.

"No way you can have any form of chocolate mixed with sprouts can you?" I was only asking myself, but Val was getting all superior.

"That is Nutella. That's the way it comes" she said in a voice which meant "surely you know that." She continued. "This is why I predict disaster."

My faith in the chef was wobbling. Chocolate in a Brussels sprouts dish did indeed seem odd, but I surmised that that children would like it, however, I knew I could get the paste without chocolate on line so that was it. That's where I would go.

Halfway to the checkout, she checked the contents of the trolley.

"Aren't you're missing something?"

I checked my list. "No. Everything is there that should be – all ticked off." Worryingly she still had that air of knowing more than I did.

"What about the Brussels sprouts?"

"Ah ... Oh." I had not put them on the list as it was so obvious I would need them that it did not seem necessary. "Oops!" was all I could think of to say. High ground back to Val.

"Just as well I came then" she opined with a deadpan face. Suffice it to say she was to keep that deadpan face all the way home. It was most irritating – as I guess it was meant to be.

Ready to Go!

I used the self service check-out. I don't know if someone was having a little joke with customers, but the loudspeaker at the till was the loudest I'd ever heard. "MORRISON'S MORE CARD ACCEPTED" It belted out. "Alright, alright" I muttered.

"SURPRISING ITEM ON THE BAGGING SCALE" was its next broadcast. I froze and cringed, I can't remember in which order. It was the Brussels sprouts. This almost stopped the shop as so many people craned their necks to see what we had put there. I shamefacedly put them into our bag as quickly as possible when we managed to get the pack through.

I felt that everybody was talking about us as we left.

"Look – there they go. They're the ones that bought Brussels sprouts." Perhaps they were whispering behind their hands. Perhaps tutting and shaking their heads. Maybe thinking "Poor man. I bet she made him buy them. Surely they won't force children to eat them."

I just crept back to the car as quickly as possible, confidence in my project having been shattered by the chocolate controversy, Val predicting disaster, bullying by the checkout tannoy, pitied by all and sundry, and the suspicion that Val might be trying to kill me.

Just to finish it off, someone had parked beside me in the car park.

On Behalf of Children at Christmas – Part 2
(December 2020)

There are times in life when everything goes just right. Well today was one of those days. Christmas decorations all up and looking splendid, Val on the sofa safely ensconced in a Christmas film and me in the kitchen, glass of wine at the ready, seasonal music playing in the background and enjoying cooking. Happiness abounded.

All ingredients measured out, neatly in pots in a line (OCD at work again) so nothing was likely to go wrong...and didn't!

Mayonnaise with the added chestnut turned out fine, sprouts shallow fried strictly in accordance with the recipe. My faith in the chef was now fully restored, and I now plated up (I think that is the technical term, the one they use on the cookery programmes). It looked just the part.

"Children everywhere will thank you for this chef" I thought. "We could call it "The acceptable face of Brussels sprouts."

It had a certain ring about it, although I had a suspicion that the phrase had been used somewhere before.

I called Val in and we were ready for the taste test.

We tasted it together.

There was silence. She looked at me. I looked at her. I thought that as the independent judge she should speak first.

"You know, when I first heard about this recipe I predicted disaster." She was expressionless. "Well I was wrong!"

More silence. Then...

"It was worse than that. It is the most totally disgusting thing I think I have ever tasted. How could it even be possible for hazelnut mayonnaise and sprouts to go together? What were you thinking!"

I was in no position to argue, because I totally agreed with her. This really was beyond the pale. The mayonnaise was so overpowering it completely overtook the taste of the sprouts, which is what I hoped for, but so not in a good way. It was so rich and sickly that even half a spoonful was too much. It was consigned to the bin and my latest food mission was scuppered.

Did the editor of the paper actually taste the recipe before publishing it? Did the chef actually taste it? I think not!

Well I hope you Mr. Editor and you the chef are happy! As a result children everywhere will be forced to continue to eat Brussels sprouts, and as for my part, I will be forced to put up with Val being impossibly superior all over Christmas.

My mother used to make cheese at home when I was very young. It seemed mystical to me how she managed to turn milk solid, and as I remember she used to hang it in some sort of fine net over the bath on a line. I was very young at the time and I guess I might have misremembered, however it seemed to me to be another string to the bow for the aspiring lockdown chef – cheesemaking...

Cheese – Part One *(February 2021)*

"The Times They Are A-Changin'" sang Bob Dylan in 1963, and I guess that it is as true now as it was then. However I would add my own footnote – but not always in a good way.

Take for instance online ordering and banking. Now in the old days, I remember being able to buy any item I took a fancy to, ignoring the budget, and not having to account for it.

I would hide it in a cupboard, and at a suitable time, as Val was passing, pretend to clear the cupboard out.

"Just found this while tidying up the cupboard" I would mention. "Don't remember it at all, we must have got it for some reason I suppose. Any ideas?"

"Can't help you there" she would reply "I don't remember it either."

Job done!

As Dylan says – times change. I decided that I would like to make home-made cheese. I wasn't sure how this would go down so I quietly ordered some equipment off the internet, which I must say was pricey and would make any cheese I made somewhat expensive. Would I be able to use my previous subterfuge to disguise my purchase?

That wasn't going to happen! This morning she was checking her banking transactions online and at the same time took a look at the joint account. She looked like she was puzzling over an entry. If you remember the film "All The Presidents Men" about the Watergate Scandal, the memorable quote from the film was "Follow the money" ...and that is exactly what she did. She had looked at my e-mails and spotted the invoice from the supplier for a cheese making kit. OK well not quite Watergate but I suppose we could call it "Cheesegate."

"You are going to make cheese then?" she enquired quizzically. "I've tried your cloggy salt, sunken bread cauliflower puree and lobster soup, sorry, bisque... so why not cheese!"

"Thought I'd give it a go" I replied nervously, at the same time quietly making a mental note to change my password.

"Can I just say that cheesemaking isn't easy, I do think it's best left to the people who know what they are doing. There are plenty of cheeses I don't like, and seeing the price of the equipment, are you sure you should be doing this?"

"Well, it's too late now - I have bought all the necessary items, and I'm going to have a crack at it. Cost effective wise, well OK that side of things doesn't look too good I agree." I was on the back foot there.

I checked my own banking. I sat and looked at the joint account. "Hang on a minute – what is that entry for a payment to "Seasalt? Do you know anything about this?" I asked.

"Ah well," came the sheepish reply. "You see it was like this – my old shoulder bag was wearing out, and I needed to replace it. It was 'half price' in the sale so I ordered it hoping you wouldn't notice. You wouldn't have in the old days you know. I would have just produced it from my wardrobe and if you'd asked, I'd just have said "Oh I've had that for ages – you must have seen it before."

She was right – I wouldn't have noticed.

You see – all this would have been avoided in Bob Dylan's day. So he was right about change but not all change is necessarily good. For either of us. It seems that both parcels are due to be delivered on Monday. Should be interesting.

Cheese − Part Two *(February 2021)*

"So what cheese do you want?" I enquired. "The book says 'Around the World in 20 Cheeses, and to give you examples, there is Labneh from Lebanon, Curd Cheese from Canada, Brunost from Norway, Bryndza from Romania, Panneer from India...''

"What about something I have even heard of" interrupted Val. "Say, Cheddar."

"It's not on their list" I admitted. "What about Cheshire − they've got that as the cheese from the UK and after all it also begins with a C." I can't believe I said that. Like it was any qualification.

"Cheshire then, but why didn't you choose a supplier who deals in British cheeses anyway? I mean, 'Cheese Monkey'? The name should have put you off. Why them?"

Easy, that one - "They were the cheapest" I replied. Surely that had to command approval I thought.

"Hmph! The whole world and she chooses Cheshire" I muttered to myself − still, I suspected, but didn't mention that I was not that confident of producing any of them anyway.

"Perhaps you should have checked that the recipes were local?" One of those comments disguised as a question. She was right of course. I should have.

"What about 'Greek Grilling Cheese'?" I ventured. I quoted verbatim from the booklet. "It says 'The reason why it squeaks when you eat it is that the protein chains you create are like tiny molecular springs that bounce against your teeth.' Tempting?"

Val was less than enthusiastic. "I like to think I am keeping up with all the modern trends" she replied, "but I am quite happy if my food does not talk back to me. Let's stick with the Cheshire."

I asked Val if she could order 1.5 l. of milk; 250 ml. of creme fraich and 250 ml. of cream.

"They've made a mistake with our order." I was looking at 4 litres of milk and 2 lots of the rest. "They've doubled everything." They didn't usually make that sort of mistake.

"Er... well no, that's actually right. I ordered double of everything because I didn't think things would go too well first time, given your track record."

"Harsh" I responded, "but probably fair comment."

Onwards and upwards – the mixture was heated, rennet added, and in due course sieved, my own Holywell Bay sea salt (Yeay!) added, squeezed, and finally a block of cheese was shaped in a pot and left to mature for oh... a least an hour.

Triumphantly I produced the result. "All done and not one mistake, despite your doubts" I announced. "Time for a taste test I think."

Before...   **...and after**

Val tasted and considered. A pause, then "Hmm..." Nothing was said because she was trying to be positive, but I took it to mean "You know the main features of Cheshire cheese? It has a dense crumbly texture, a sharp style and a salty taste. Those features are... well... sort of there, but perhaps not so much?"

"Well...er.. OK it's texture is definitely of cream cheese, definitely mellow bordering on bland, and definitely not a hint of salt" was my take on it. Even I thought I'd be breaking the Trades Description Act if I called it Cheshire.

I referred to page three of the instruction booklet. My faith in the Cheese Monkey was wobbling.

"See here, it says 'Remember, even if things don't go exactly how you planned you will still end up with cheese, just not necessarily the cheese you were intending to make!' and you must admit it does have a general cheeselike quality. What I'll do is let it mature in the 'fridge for a month or so and with a bit of luck it'll harden."

Val thought for a moment. "Fair enough, but can I just point out that Christmas has just come and gone. We had enough cheese to feed the family. As that didn't happen due to Covid I already have carload of cheese left over in the 'fridge."

"Now you tell me" I thought.

I think that despite my new found expertise as a chef (my assessment) sometimes I had to bow to greater knowledge and was put firmly in my place.

Kitchen Initiative *(March 2021)*

I have come to think over the years that we have struck a reasonable balance regarding kitchen duties. Val does the clever stuff like the cooking, and I carry out the more mundane chores such as cleaning up the kitchen after the meal. This seems to balance out at around 50/50 so all is well.

Today I thought I'd lend a hand cooking and using my initiative, would surprise her with some help with the meal.

"What's for dinner?" I asked, matter-of-factly.

"Peri Peri chicken with a lovely salad. It was with the Waitrose delivery and was quite expensive, but I think you'll enjoy it." came the reply.

Now I had no idea what the Peri Peri bit was but chicken sounded good to me. I also thought that ordering a delivery from Waitrose was us getting above our station in life, but on the plus side it might wind up the neighbours.

Val retrieved it from the 'fridge and left it on the side. She then disappeared to... well I didn't know to do what, but I took my chance to start to help and removed it from it's plastic bag. She returned carrying various salad items.

"What are you doing?" she enquired, in my opinion rather too loudly, which was not what I was expecting.

"I've decided to help with the dinner." I was beaming from ear to ear. "I'm using my initiative and I've made a start by getting the chicken ready for the oven. What can I do next?" I was into it now.

"Well you can go back into the other room for a start" was the last answer I was expecting to hear.

"Bit harsh" I thought. "Nothing wrong is there?"

"There just might be" was the reply, "did you read the instructions?"

"No, but if there is a problem it's probably nothing I can't sort out – I said that I am here to help".

"OK – how do I get the chicken back in the specially sealed bag, there to ensure the flavour is retained, and bake it in the oven – like it says on the front of the bag?" I mean, what were you thinking!

I immediately cancelled all thoughts of using my initiative and retreated from the kitchen as instructed leaving Val scratching her head.

I decided that I would use this as a learning curve on my way to chef mastery. This lesson learned would be: "read the instructions."

"Also maybe I'll stick to the clearing up for a while... I'm not as far forward in my cooking career as I thought" I concluded silently.

Sometimes things found on the internet can leave me speechless...

Am I That Old? *(March 2021)*

I like to think that pushing 72, I am keeping up with the modern way of life. I can do Zoom. I have installed Netflix on my TV. I'm in the process of installing the app. on my 'phone which pays for things direct.

But on the odd occasion I suddenly feel my age. Saturday mornings in our household consists of reading, cover to cover an improving newspaper with copious amounts of tea and toast, which OK, is pure oldie. Then suddenly something catches my eye that really does makes me realise how old I am.

This morning I read that Gwyneth Paltrow has marketed a candle called – and I quote exactly "This Smells Like My Vagina." (If you don't believe me - Google it!). Well clearly she has totally lost her marbles, but she is a superstar and the majority of them go bonkers sooner or later.

But wait – and this is the "world's gone mad" bit. They are £60 a pop, and she has sold out!   See – I'm just living in a past world.

....or maybe not. Perhaps Val and I can get in on the act.

In the past I have had occasion to rant about underarm deodorant. But now we're going to work on a liquid version of pure BO and as soon as it is perfected, we are going to patent it. We'll then send a sample for Miss Paltrow to test and market it for me at, say 20% of the profit.

If we call it "This smells like my armpit" I'm thinking, at least £50 a bottle? We can then just let the money roll in!

Not actually to do with lockdown – it just makes me laugh!

Wedding Anniversary *(April 2021)*

"Our anniversary is coming up and can you remember when it was?"

This is this annual test I get, and I don't know whether it is to covertly remind me of the date or whether I am being tested to check to see if I can remember the date. Either way I am sensing danger.

These days though I am older and wiser - I have in the past fallen foul of this question by being unable to remember the actual date, so I am replying today "Well it's the 12th of April of course." This was memorised from times years ago when I was taken to task in no small way for not remembering, leading to much trauma. Both brownie points and kudos (got that from Strava) earned and given means that I am now considering the matter closed.

I am in the loft, searching for something, I can't remember what, but I can never find what I am looking for up there anyway. I stumble across the nostalgia box containing basically our life to date. Guessing most people have one. As always, it stops me in my tracks and I spend half an hour re-living our past as I wade through all the pointless items we have kept.

Suddenly I spot the invoice from the Minto House Hotel at Pentire (long since demolished) where we had our wedding buffet in 1990. Val will be interested in this I am thinking, as I excitedly rush to find her.

"Look what I have found! Didn't know we had kept this." I wait to see Val's reaction to the memory of our big day. We are now studying it together, misty eyed and re-living the moment. As I look I am noticing something odd.

"I see this is dated 14th April" I say. Now we didn't have the reception two days later, so we are now scratching our heads.

"I've got it" says Val. "We paid for it on the Monday and that's the reason for the date – it was when the invoice was issued."

That seems fine to me, but just to check I am looking now at "timeanddate.com" which tells you what day it was given any date in the past. I am typing in 14th April 1990. Turns out it's the Saturday.

Silence.

"Oh My God" we exclaim in unison – "all these years we have been celebrating on the wrong date – including our 30[th.]"

I am now in my being impossibly superior mood. "So all this time I have been taken to task for not remembering our anniversary and you've got the wrong date?" This is not a question (despite the question mark) and I'm only just getting started.

I am enjoying the deafening silence which is long and I am wallowing in my righteousness when Val asks "How's the family history going?"

"Ha!" I am thinking. I always start with that when I am on the high ground. "Ha! She is changing the subject." It has been my hobby for many years.

"I am way back to the early 1700's" I say "...and I have been meticulous in my researches with dates, places and occupations. I am quite proud of it. I was only looking at it today."

"So, all the way to you?"

"Yes."

Sometimes it is the most obvious things that can completely pass you by. You should clearly see it coming but for an unaccountable reason you miss it. Safe to say I am oblivious to this oncoming juggernaut.

"So am I on your chart?"

"Yes of course are – right here at the bottom of the line – it lists our wed... Oh!...Erm...Ah!" I am interrupted.

"...and what date do you have there?" A question that was not a question. This time the silence is even more deafening than the last. I mutter something indecipherable.

"So, really you've known all along it was the 14th."

The high ground is still there but it's not me on it, and I am finding that a one-all draw is only a good result when you equalise, not when you score first.

"You know my daughter thinks we are a pair of prize plonkers" says Val later after we have fully digested our mistake and Val clearly having told her.

"Perhaps – but I think she always has" I reply. "So what do we do about this?" I ask.

Silence, then... "I think we should wait until Wednesday, open a bottle of Champagne and sit on the floor giggling about it all afternoon."

"Good plan" I reply.

Once again we had a bout of watching television as lockdown had been extended by the Government – but as I was now well into my cooking we were now going to try a joint effort - with each other - and Marcus Wareing

Bangers and Mash *(April 2021)*

The celebrity culture is with us to stay. It seems that you embrace it or you ignore it completely, there being no half measures. I have chosen the latter and I have a rule that I will never watch anything on the television that contains the word "celebrity."

This also includes programmes where celebrities just do things for their own enjoyment. Examples are like celebrities climbing hills, going sailing, fishing, train trips and the like. This is because, in effect, you are now watching someone just living their life – but also they are getting paid for it, whilst you are sitting there with your own life slipping by.

Then down the slippery slope you go, so that in the end you are watching someone who is not even a celebrity live their life on screen.

So what has this got to do with bangers and mash?

Well, Val was watching Masterchef, and celebrity chef Marcus Wareing produced it as a skills test last week. To be fair he was actually acting as a chef, which is what he is famous for, so on reflection, as he wasn't cycling from Land's End to John O'Groats, it was OK to watch, and nothing to do with the above, which is just one of my rants – apologies for that.

All Set!

The point of this was that Val was so enthused, that today appeared free range pork sausages, red and white onions, Guinness, brandy, butter, balsamic vinegar, honey and Maris Piper potatoes on the kitchen work surface.

"This is tonight's dinner" she announced. "Not just bangers and mash, it is Masterchef bangers and mash."

"Not sure that quote hasn't been thought of already" I noted, also not being sure of my role in this project.

We have a small television on the wall of the kitchen, and we have Sky TV. However, I'm too mean to have their multiroom option which costs extra, so we could not follow the programme direct from the screen. In order to copy what he did, we decided Val should play the section of the programme in the lounge and call out what I should do in the kitchen as it went along. It seemed a good idea at the time. She had also made a list.

"Right. Start by reducing the Guinness in a pan."

"How much Guinness?" I queried.

"He didn't say."

"Good start" I thought, and went into the lounge to watch the replay. "Half a can it looks like."

"Then slice and caramelise the onions."

"How many onions?"

"He didn't say."

"Right. This is getting silly. I'm just going to guess from now on." I sliced two red and two white onions, which on reflection was way too much as I had enough to sink a battleship. Actually they did sweat down quite a bit, so I could now just about get them into the pan properly.

"Now he's adding the balsamic vinegar and wholegrain mustard."

"Hang on a minute – wholegrain mustard? No-one said anything about that. It's not on your list." I admit that I was getting a bit accusative. Worse was that despite scouring the kitchen and the garage, which doubles as a grocery shop, there was none to be found.

"Oh just bung some French mustard in instead." Was I mistaken or was Val too getting a bit short now?

"Not sure about that" I replied. "I'll leave the mustard."

"He's now frying the sausages, gently so as to get an even brownness. It's with a spring of the Rosemary....or was it the Thyme?" came the call from the lounge.

"Those were not on the list either" I muttered. "Do the editors of this programme not realise that people are copying this?" Luckily we had both.

Of course using both did lighten the mood, as those of us of a certain age will attest, it coerces you into singing a Simon and Garfunkel song under your breath, and which once in there, will not leave your head.

"Now add the brandy to the onions and flambe."

Val rushed into the kitchen to see what all the yelping was about.

"I've singed my fingers" I whined, my mood once again black and all thoughts of songs suddenly gone.

"Exactly how much brandy did you use?" she pointlessly queried.

"Have a guess" I growled.

"Now he's adding the stock" she called out, now back in the lounge.

I tipped some in, which made the whole concoction much darker, and quite honestly looking like something it should look like.

"Now add the Guinness."

"Eh! What do you mean... I've already added it." I thought she had scrolled the television back too far and was repeating herself in some way. "I thought the Guinness was the stock."

"No, you should have a jugful of stock – he's just tipped some of it in." Now we did scroll back, and there was the mysterious jug.

"And where was that on the list?" I said, talking to no-one at all, but imagining that Marcus was in front of me, being called to account for this omission. I was staring at him, giving him the look of Monica Galetti at her most fierce. In truth I got nowhere near it.

Back in reality, It now seemed quite clear that we were not getting the full picture from his demonstration. Is there anything darker than black? Well at that point I had just invented it, as that was the colour of my mood as I scoured the cupboard for a stock cube. We had just one left. Kettle boiled, a squeeze of honey and job done.

The Final Stages

Val appeared looking harassed.

"Tell you what – I'll help by cooking the mashed potatoes." I was guessing that she felt that relaying instructions from the other room was not going well, and she needed a change of scene.

"Brilliant" I replied. I was very happy that I had got out of cooking the mash.

With potatoes now ready, Val asked if I wanted to mash, and then pass them through the sieve.

"Yes and No" I replied. I found that beating the hell out of boiled potatoes strangely recuperating and had the added advantage of making sure there there were no lumps at all, so no need for a sieve. Butter and milk added, then sausages added to the mix on the stove, and we were ready to plate up.

Or were we? I tasted the mix. Val followed.

"It doesn't taste of anything." she said. "Could be that we have both contracted Covid-19 I suppose, but tell you what – add some more Guinness and add the French mustard and with a bit of luck, that'll pep it up a bit."

It certainly made it look darker, richer and actually it was now tastier. "I'll just add some baked beans to the meal as well" she decided.

What I have learned. Masterchef is all about the competition, and is not geared up for copying.

What has Val learned. Do not say "Well Marcus Wareing only took twenty minutes to do that."

On 17th May the Government allowed pubs to reopen with the rule of six. We were very quick to take advantage of this ruling.

Sunday Lunch *(May 2021)*

We were at our table at The Smugglers Den today

"...so what I objected to most was the way he was being interviewed on the programme - it showed a complete disrespect for...." I tailed off as Val was looking away.

"What are you doing?"

"Oh - I was just listening to the customer on the next table - he was ordering Sunday lunch."

"Why?"

"Well it was more interesting..."

Silence ensued!

With our new freedoms now well embedded into our everyday life I was thinking that we could have done better than strawberry picking. However...

Strawberry Fields *(June 2021)*

"Let's go strawberry picking - the fields have just opened" said Val.

"Why don't we just go to Morrison's and buy some?"

"They'll be much tastier and the sun's out."

"...and it'll be fun."

"Really?"

We arrived at the fields.

"Oh look - they've got some picked in punnets already - job done!" I said hopefully.

"No - they are £2 per kilo. more expensive - we're going picking.

And we did.

We bought 1.5 kilo's worth which saved £3. There were two of us so that meant I worked for 20 minutes saving £1.50. That's £4.50 per hour. The minimum wage is £8.21. Who knew that when I retired I would be put back to work at a rate of £4.50 per hour.

It's a disgrace!

Despite our yearning to get out and about now that we were allowed to, domestic chores were still never far away.

The Duvet Ritual *(June 2021)*

"Ray, have you got a minute?"

This was the call from Val which I know has to come but always dread, because it never ends well. It is the ritual of changing the duvet cover. Today was worse as it was changing the duvet itself from winter to summer – something to do with TOGs I believe. It stands for thermal resistance and in my world that would be TR but I guess that would be way too simple and I still don't know what TOG stands for.

Anyway back to the matter in hand.

"It's way too hot to have the winter duvet on, so we need to change it." Val was being very authoritative.

"I'll get it out of the loft. I'll be a few minutes." In turn, I was trying to be very supportive.

"If you remember I said put it near the front." She was correct of course but that was last September and since then everything she has wanted to put up there apparently also needed to be at the front, and that included all the Christmas decorations. It was now at the back.

I considered it a job for Pickfords, there was so much to move around up there, and as it was not fully boarded I had to be somewhat careful where I put my feet, sundry boxes, items of furniture and many boxes of business accounts as the VAT people wanted us to keep them for ten years, I'm guessing just to annoy us as there was no way they would ever ask us to produce them now.

So finally I appeared with the 4.5 TOG duvet, triumphant but dusty.

"That'll teach you not to put it at the back" Val observed dryly.

I couldn't think of anything to say, but was certain that if I had thought of something it would have been equally dry.

Now the easy bit. Off with the old duvet, separate from it's cover, duvet into the bag for the laundry and the cover flung down the stairs for washing, which was strangely satisfying.

Things deteriorated from here. The whole project of getting the duvet into the cover was more than a little difficult as the hole for it covered less than half the end of the cover. This seemed to me to be bizarre to say the least as it seemed pointlessly small. Also Val decided that it would be a race to see which of us could get the duvet into the corner of the cover first which ended up in a wrestling match which I lost.

"Why is the hole so ridiculously small anyway?" I complained. "It has no buttons either – how do you do it up?"

"Because it's French – and you don't" explained Val. This was as far as I was concerned, a less than adequate explanation.

"Well why did you by a French cover?"

"Because it was in a sale and I liked the colour." Better, but still not satisfactory.

Now, regarding the French. We in the UK are good neighbours, and when they were having a little difficulty, the friendly thing to do was to help out, which we did in not one, but two World Wars. What do they do in return? They saturate our market with cheap duvet covers, of an inferior quality with small holes and no buttons, clearly made in the sweat shops in Parisian slums using illegal immigrants and child labour, putting our linen mills out of business and our honest hard working artisans on the street, unable to feed their children.

They complained vigorously when we tried to join the Common Market and inexplicably just as vigorously when we left the European Union. Because they ignore the territorial waters despite our leaving, huge French trawlers scour the bed of the English Channel scraping it clean of any living creature leaving it looking like an underwater moonscape, at the same time as bankrupting our plucky clean living gently sustainably line fishing fishermen who only want to earn enough to keep their children in shoes and their grannies in adequately comfortable old folks homes, by blockading their ports with their boats, and even if a half dozen or so boxes of langoustines our boys caught in the UK/England (depending on the next independence referendum) get past this, they will be kept for two weeks in a hot shed by the French customs before sending on, only to be eventually returned anyway because of incomplete paperwork.

They like us to export our lambs to France as woolly as possible as it will be easier for the farmers to set fire to them and just in case we take to the skies there will be regular Air Traffic Control strikes, unannounced of course, to ensure compatibility with their surface travel philosophy, except on days though, when they are air freighting inferior duvet covers with small holes and no buttons. If that isn't enough, they then rub our noses in it by showing us how to win the World Cup.

In return the UK, as a fine upstanding example of how a country should behave, will let more inferior duvet covers in without hindrance, tariffs and paperwork on lorries full of the same illegal immigrants who made them tucked in the back for good measure.

Actually I didn't say that, I just thought it. Meanwhile Val continued.
"On balance I must say that I quite like the French. Remember when we had that weekend away in Paris, every French person

we spoke to was charming, and remember that guy who went out of his way to ensure we found the correct Metro station by leading us right up to it?" She had a point.

"You are right of course, the French are a very agreeable bunch" I concurred. Probably just as well she can't mind read.

"...and we had a really comfortable hotel room, we definitely had no problem with the duvet or the cover there, did we. Also the French invented the duvet – did you know that?"

"Well we didn't have to change that one did we." I responded, the mask nearly slipping.

"Anyway, when it comes back from the laundry, we'll need it again in September, so when you put it back in the loft, can you make sure that you put it near the front."

With most restrictions now lifted, life was getting back to normal although the wearing of masks was still necessary. We were now venturing out further, but on this occasion only got as far as the bay.

Val's Shirley Valentine Moment *(July 2021)*

Val was watching a film called "Shirley Valentine", the plot of which is apparently a housewife, bored with her downtrodden life decides to escape to a Greek island where, without all the restrictions of an everyday life, she can "find her real self".

Notice how I say "apparently" in order to convey the impression that I wasn't watching it as well, which secretly I was. Anyway this lady ends up borrowing a chair and table from a local taverna and sits with a glass and a bottle of wine on the beach staring out at the sunset, presumably having done exactly what she wanted to do – finding her real self.

The film ended.

"Ray... I was thinking."

"Oh dear – yes?" I said enquiringly.

"Thing is, it's getting on for 8 o'clock, it's gloriously sunny and there has to be a wonderful sunset coming. I would like to sit by the sea with a glass of wine and watch it set. What do you think?"

"I think you've been watching too many films" was my rather inadequate answer, knowing however that the die had been cast.

I was laden with two chairs, a full bottle of wine, two wine glasses wrapped for protection, and coat as we were going to be

there some time. "You do know the car park is half a mile from the beach" I complained.
"Quarter of a mile at most" she replied.

"Oh that's alright then" was my only answer, which again on reflection was inadequate. "You know in the film, they carried the stuff just across the road" I added, pointlessly.

We reached Holywell Bay beach, and because of the sand dunes in the way, to get to the sea involved a trek over them or round them, either way not conducive to those laden down.

"This looks like a good place" I said before we started.

"Oh no – it's got to be by the sea" came the reply.

"Of course it has – silly me." Can't remember whether I said it or just thought it as we finally reached the high tide mark. It was nowhere near high tide.

"In the film it was high tide" Val pointed out. I gazed at the distant ocean despondently. Surely no further.

"The tide is coming in, so no point in going on" I said hopefully, and to my delight we made camp there. Chairs out, wine poured and to be fair a great sunset ensued. It was very enjoyable.

Val was gazing out to sea. "Have you found your real self?" I asked innocently and with a bit of luck, annoyingly.

"I think this is wonderful" came the reply. "Almost perfect."

"What do you mean – almost?"

"Well, you forgot to bring the table."

On the 19th July we were advised that the requirement to wear masks had been relaxed. We also had relaxed our own more stringent self-imposed lockdown conditions and Val decided we would now really go for it.

Out to Lunch *(July 2021)*

"The weather looks gorgeous for the next few days, it's perfect for a lunch out – in a garden overlooking the sea." This was the conclusion by Val as she looked at the forecast. I had this picture in my mind of a five minute journey to the Bowgie, half an hour to comprehend their ultra covid-safe ordering system, have lunch and back by around two. Perfect, I thought. Yes – let's do it!

"Juliet's Garden I'm thinking, What about on Tuesday?"

"Eh? What?" My plan scuppered before it had even started.

The award winning Juliet's Garden is in an idyllic spot. It has firmly established itself as a popular and highly attractive restaurant, boasting breathtaking views across the local harbour. Ideal for what Val wanted.

However, here is the drawback. We are talking over four hours on the way there and the same on the way back. It is situated on the Isles of Scilly. But with the weather set fair...well why not.

The ferry leaves Penzance at 9.15 and booking in needs to be at least an hour earlier. Having done this before we know that you have to get there at least 7.30 if you want the best seats on the boat. This is why we were travelling down the Camborne Bypass at sometime around 6.30.

Maybe because it was so early or maybe it was because there was nothing else on the road, we started tractor counting. On the dual carriageway I counted eight going east. Were they being stolen and taken to Eastern Europe by organised crime? Were they heading for the channel ports to blockade the plethora of French lorries in retaliation for them upsetting our fishermen? Were they congregating at the border at Launceston to repel the invading emmets? Well one can only hope.

The harbour car park at Penzance costs £8 for the day. Here's a tip though – the Western Prominade Road has totally free parking on the sea front, and the only problem is finding a space, even at 7 am. There was one. Only one, but that was enough. Local knowledge, see!

We were there before 7am, an hour too early. The Queuing Marshal said that we could not queue until 7.30 but to wait on the other side of the road and he would give us the nod when it was time. So in effect, we queued in the queue to join the queue.

On board, every twenty minutes or so we were told over the Tannoy that we had to wear our masks. Upper deck, lower deck or outside, it didn't matter – mask up! And everyone did. A great deal of muttering ensued as the Government's freedom day had just passed by.

Suddenly the Tannoy came back to life. "Passengers have told us that it is now no longer a requirement to wear masks."

Mutiny!

Was the ship the new HMS Bounty? Was the ghost of Captain Bligh haunting the Bridge? Would those wearing masks be manhandled into the lifeboats and set adrift? Would "Mutiny on the Scillonian" be made into a film?

Hands were grasping the masks. Already ears were being unhooked. Clearly sides would need to be taken. We decided we would be on the side of "masks on" and risk it as I knew what had happened to Fletcher Christian and his mutineers and it did not end well. The air of expectancy was palpable.

But then "... the wearing of masks is a condition of carriage. Masks must be worn."

Never in the history of the crossing could there have been such a collective air of disappointment. Hands dropped to sides. Ears were hooked up again. Shoulders were hunched and passengers were gazing out to sea where freedom lay, so near but yet so far. The mutiny was crushed.

A tad over two and a half hours later, approaching St. Mary's, once again the Tannoy sprang to life. "Passengers are requested to stay in their seats until called, in order that we can ensure passengers are disembarked safely in a Covid secure manner." This was announced twice so they were serious and we surmised that it could take quite some time.

What actually happened was that they put a rope across the gangway while they moored up, and then took it away again.

...and that was it.

More than 450 passengers just made a beeline for the exit, luckily for us we were near the front and were off in seconds. There was an almighty crush behind us, a "superspreader" event waiting to happen. I wondered if how much mayhem would be caused if someone coughed in the middle.

At the end of St. Mary's there was a sign saying "Three Bays and a Hill to Juliet's Garden." Each one was more beautiful than the one before. The walk was idyllic, although we kept being passed by people route marching. We knew what they were doing. They were after the best tables at the restaurant, but in doing so missed the whole point of being on the Island.
No booking at JG's – it's first come first served. "Could we have a table with a parasol please?" I asked.

"I'm sorry, all those are taken I'm afraid" said the waiter. We don't have enough to cover all the tables."

"Perhaps then get some more?" I muttered.

Luckily one couple left and a table for eight became free ....with a parasol nearby. "Can I have that parasol?" I asked a waitress.

"You'll have to move it" came the response. "Fine by me" I thought, and did.

"What would you like to drink?" she continued.

"A glass of Prosecco and a cider please – what is the cider by the way?"

"We have Rattler or Rolling Apples on draught."

"Rolling Apples – not heard of that one before, what's it like?"

"Well it's an apple cider" came the response, and she departed to deal with the order. I was waiting for her to say "innit" afterwards. She was of the age, but she didn't. I was strangely disappointed.

"Hmm... I bet If I'd asked for a Tarquin's gin she'd have waxed lyrical" (Sorry). Why don't youngsters go for cider anyway?

"Two crab baguettes please" we ordered from the waiter.

"I'm sorry, it's after one and all the crab is gone, you have to get here early to order crab."

"Perhaps then get some more?" I muttered.
So the route marchers had cleaned the place out. Well I hoped they all boiled as they raced up the hill in this heat.

"Prawn baguette it is then."

The waitress came back with the drinks. She was absolutely right, the cider was just a perfectly ordinary everyday apple cider – nothing original about it all, much like a "Thatchers", but to be fair there is nothing wrong with that. The baguettes were of course, delicious.

The couple on the next table had gone and left the remains of a cream tea. One thing about JG's is the tameness of the sparrows. Immediately they had left, the remains were set upon in a scene reminiscent of Hitchcock's "The Birds." Nervously we looked up just to check that the seagulls weren't massing for an attack.

"So what do you think?" I asked.

"It'll be OK" replied Val, "I've every confidence." We waited. I crossed my fingers and wondered what would happen.

There was no need to worry, they were Cornish birds and of course they went for the jam first. ...although actually they went for the crumbs first, then the jam – but it was before the cream and that's what counts. Not actually sure if they went for the cream at all.

Time to leave and as we got up a couple dived for the table.

"Are you leaving, only we're desperate for a table with a parasol."

"All yours" we replied.

He considered the shortage of parasols.

"Perhaps then get some more?" he mused.
Ambling down to Porthloo, the first of the three bays, we looked over to the harbour in the distance. It was not yet 3.00

and passengers were queueing to get back on the boat, presumably to bag the best seats. It didn't leave until 4.30. We just continued to paddle on our calm and tranquil beach.

A couple passed us. I was envious of them in that this was their first visit to the islands and they were entranced. I remember that feeling, there is nothing like the first visit. I changed my mind about being envious though when they said they were going back to Biggleswade. Can't really comment because I've never been to Biggleswade, but I just feel it's a place to come from rather than go to.

Back on board, all the outside seats had gone to the route marchers, only now, hopefully, as well as boiling, they were over bloated with the crab which would serve them right. We settled down in a quiet shady spot feeling superior.

Along the Camborne Bypass we were counting tractors again. That didn't take much effort as there were only two. But where were the rest? Were they still at the front, fighting the French? Had they relocated to the Tamar Bridge to block emmets slipping though that way? We decided that they were now well on their way to Eastern Europe having been stolen by organised crime.

"You asked a lot of questions today" said Val as we pulled up to the house.

" I have another" I replied. "When can we go again?"

Now we were really out and about – but at the same time it provided an opportunity at my age for a little nostalgia.

Addiction *(July 2021)*

I think at my time of life, when days are spent reflecting on times past and particularly the days of my youth I look back at the mistakes I made and wonder if I had known then what I know now, would I have changed things?

I admit now I had succumbed to an addiction. It started slowly, insidiously, and seductively without me really noticing it, until one day my family took me aside and tried to wean me off it. Shockingly it was complete news to me, I did not know I was ensnared, but in the cold light of day I realised that I was completely trapped in a nightmare.

I knew that on so many Friday nights I, and other similarly addicted victims would meet by the underpass at Waterloo Station in London to indulge our wild fantasies. We would spend the whole weekend away from our families with no feeling of guilt at all. I used to manage to get myself straight again for work on Monday, but I knew that it would be only too soon before I would again give in to my addiction. There seemed to be no escape. So now, after all these years I admit it.

I was an addicted peak bagger.

It started so innocently. I had a girlfriend at the time who lived in Bexley in Kent. One day she took me to Shooter's Hill in Greenwich. In passing she said that it was 433ft. high and was the 10th highest point in London. I think this was the beginning and I can blame Janet for my downfall, because quite naturally I wanted to know what the highest point was, which after examination of OS maps appeared to be Stanmore Hill in Harrow, 499ft. It had to be done of course and only days later I could boast of being the highest person in London – the top half of me being satisfyingly 500 feet up. There were those who would say that Westerham Heights, at 804 ft. was higher, but that's in Kent, and to me doesn't count. I bagged it anyway just in case.

It was not long before I went for a bigger and bigger fix. 2,000 footers on Dartmoor and later the Peak District. The disappointment of finding that Pen-y-fan in the Brecon Beacons was only 2,900ft. meant that I now needed the hard stuff.

The mini-bus by the underpass at Waterloo Station took us on many expeditions to the 3,000 footers. In the end we bagged the then 14 Welsh 3,000s all of which ended up on my list.

Even this was not enough. We eventually were ticking off Scottish 4,000 foot Munros. But it was not just the high peaks, any hill with a spot height and a name was fair game. The list of names was now impossible to manage, but my employers, seeing the trouble I was in took pity on me and moved me away from temptation by sending me to Newquay. If not I would have been still stuck on that treadmill.

New life, with small children, as far away from the mountains as possible allowed me to defeat this addiction. But I had still kept the lists so I knew I could easily slip back and to be honest here have been a couple of lapses since. I added St Agnes Beacon, Rough Tor and Brown Willy to the list before I managed to check my downward spiral.

There was that time we had to turn off the M5 in Somerset just to climb Brent Knoll. Worst of all we drove to the Midlands to climb The Wrekin. I mean – you can almost drive up it – we had to walk it!

Now in my later years I feel that I have managed to defeat this need to find new peaks to climb. But it never leaves me totally, I still have the lists tucked away somewhere.

So why bring it up now?

Ah well, it was all bought into focus yesterday on Trevose Head. I spied a trig. point on a small hill I hadn't seen before. Before I knew it myself I was there. It was 74 metres high. Wouldn't be a problem if I just added it to my list I thought, and took a couple of photographs.

Trig. Point No. S1755

These days we have the internet, and it couldn't harm if I just saw if there were any other people interested in trig. points. How could that possibly hurt? Well, I found www.trigbagging.co.uk and it has a map.

Sorry Valerie but I'm already plotting our next expedition. I am back on the treadmill. There is no hope.

Life being back to normal meant that we could celebrate our birthdays and anniversaries properly again – but some pubs having instigated a covid safe system of booking were loath to let it go.

The Birthday *(August 2021)*

"Well I blame my mother."

That was my considered conclusion after a fruitless search to find a venue for my 73rd birthday which was imminent.

A distinct lack of forward planning. No thoughts of the difficulties that are faced by August children in later years when trying to celebrate occasions in the height of the summer holidays. You can't get in anywhere and even if you can, everything is twice the price it would be in September, I mean, why didn't she wait?"

I was on a roll. "We had the good sense to have children in June, September and October, giving them cheap hotel, restaurant and pub options. I hope they are suitably grateful."

"Hang on a minute though. Wasn't our own first date on 31st August?" said Val. "You only had a week to wait to ask me out and our own anniversaries would have been so much cheaper!"

Hmm.. perhaps I took after my mother more than I thought.

"...so perhaps you took after your mother more than you thought" she continued.

Online we finally found a venue where we could book but it was for outside and there didn't seem to be an inside option. This seemed strange but there seemed no way to do this, so we telephoned them. They were not taking telephone calls.

"OK" I said, "it's just down the road, we'll just call in and book."
At the desk we explained the problem to the receptionist.

"That's right" she said. "We take bookings online for an outside table."

"Can we have an inside table."

"We don't take bookings for those."

"So how do we get one?"

"You don't. They are not available."

"Why not?"

"They are reserved for the outside tables in case it rains, so that they have the option to come inside. Where would they all go if all the inside tables were full?"

"But we already want the option to come inside."

"So you must book an outside table and choose the option to come inside if it rains. Have you not read our web site instructions all the way through? It says that if it rains you can come inside."

"So what happens if it doesn't rain?"

"Ah well, we will offer you the option to come inside if it doesn't rain."

"So whether or not it rains we can come inside, although to be fair the website does not say that – why don't you just confirm that now, we will take that option and come inside."

"Because you can only book an outside table on our website, not with me. Have you not read our website instructions all the way through?"

"I think you've said that already."

"Well no-one else has had a problem."

"Perhaps they didn't want an inside table."

We worked out that each booking had reserved for them an outside table and an inside table, but you could only book the outside one, even though you wanted the inside table. They would then transfer you if it rained. They would also transfer you if it didn't rain.

The logic of all this did actually escape me and also it certainly did not seem to me to be the best use of resources.

We decided, as the atmosphere was now quite frosty, that we would reconsider our options and as Val had briskly left the building, I thought I'd follow.

After many more enquiries using the "Open Table" app. on our computer, we were still tableless. Things seemed hopeless.

Val sent an e-mail in desperation to another venue. Five minutes later we had an e-mail back confirming a reservation for eight on Sunday.

We were really impressed with this new and an up-to-date modern system of booking a table. We worked it through in our minds. We had asked them for a table. They then booked us in and confirmed back. So simple.

"You know they have hit upon a really clever way of booking tables" I said. "I'm surprised no-one has thought of it before. It could really catch on."

With all now in place Val announced "One more thing we must do."

"What's that?"

"We must make sure all the grandchildren are aware of the pitfalls in later life of creating anniversaries of any kind in August."

"It's our duty to do so" I agreed.

Whilst garden birdwatching could be a useful pastime for most during lockdowns, sadly where we live we mainly get seagulls.

The Seagull *(August 2021)*

We've watched a seagull grow from egg to juvenile on the roof opposite us since the spring, and we've come to the conclusion that there has been some very poor parenting going on here. This chick, (there doesn't seem to be a clever name for a baby seagull) now in its teenage years, is now a deluded delinquent. There is a flat roof on the garages opposite and they regularly have a puddle after rain. We watched for a quarter of an hour today whilst this reprobate wildly attacked it's reflection again and again.

We think in the end it called it a draw as it gave up after that. It didn't stop there though. The picture above shows it tearing off rose leaves from our climbing rambler. Pure vandalism I call it.

From there it's only one step away from stealing pasties from passers by. Obviously no problem if it's from holidaymakers, but clearly the lack of discipline in its childhood will mean it won't distinguish between them and locals.

My parents wouldn't have allowed this behaviour in the 60's when I was a child. If so much as a sparrow misbehaved it would be up before the beak! (Sorry).

Not everything always goes to plan and sometimes there have to be changes.

Revenge *(August 2021)*

So it has come to this. As I see you for the last time, leaving, off to a new life with your "friend", I sit here and reflect on our relationship over the past years.

Well it's not been easy. I remember when I first saw you, looking at your best, just standing there, in a corner. There and then I knew we were destined to be together, and it seemed that in no time at all, you were living with me and we had started our exciting new relationship. I was so happy.

But how quickly things started to go wrong. It was always about money. Within weeks I was paying out on your behalf. There was always something you needed. It was always urgent, and if you didn't get it, you would end up sulking, doing nothing at all until I sorted out whatever you wanted.

This went on for years, a never ending list of things you persuaded me had to be done, bleeding me dry. Oh yes, fool that I was, I paid up, never criticising and always giving in to you.

I was looking at you recently, and I suddenly noticed that maybe you were not as attractive as you were. Perhaps a little rough around the edges? Had all this money I had spent you you been worth it? After all this time was I seeing you for what you really were? Made me wonder whether in fact, we would be together much longer.

So when last week, you were disappearing down the road with your new partner, maybe it was with a sense of relief that I would now be on my own again. I wondered if you had

actually ever cared. For my part, I suddenly realised I was happy again.
Ha! How little you know.

Let me tell you the reality. For a start I am not alone. I am already in a new relationship and I am as happy as can be. It's so easy going. Already we have been away on trips together, going shopping, and visiting family all without any difficulties or trauma.

Secondly, your friend is not who you think he is. You think that you are destined to spend the rest of your life with him, and I suppose in a sense you are, but it is going to be a short one.

He is a car dismantler. You are heading straight for the scrap yard. So WJ 05 FZX Ford Focus, your years of costing me a fortune, with so many repairs, failed MOT tests and the like, have finally caught up with you ...and how about this for a final slice of irony – he has paid me to take you away.

For obvious reasons the car did not get much use during the lockdown. Nevertheless things kept going wrong with it, culminating in the final straw when the central locking system decided it would lock us in.

Football *(August 2021)*

So, the new Premiership season is upon us.

Last year Val and I, bored with the National Lottery, decided we would use the money saved (£2 per week) to have a competition between us and we each put £1 on betting the full ten Premiership results, each week.

I would use my many years of experience of following the various teams, weighing up past and recent performance, checking on injuries, analysing the team lists each week, surveying the pundit's predictions, judging these factors against the published betting odds and arriving at a fully comprehensive forecast detailing whether the result of each game would be home, away or draw.

Val, knowing little and caring even less about football, took one look at the table each week and just picked a forecast out of the air. Clearly, this was not even a contest.

It wasn't. Val won about two thirds of the 38 rounds and once actually got them all right. There were only five matches that week but she won a couple of hundred pounds, and beat me by two that week. It could only have been a fault in the system as of course my expertise was perfectly sound.

But this is a new season and I have instigated a new fully scientific system, removing the variables, an algorithm if you like. In my opinion it cannot fail and I confidently predict that winnings will very shortly be flowing.

The fact that on one day last season Val drew her forecast out of a hat yet still beat me, is now consigned to history.

Just a little puzzled as to why my system didn't work in the first week.

By now my months of research during lockdown resulted in me considering myself to be a cookery expert. So I was raring to go with a new venture, and as luck would have it my chance came sooner than I expected.

It's Hollandaise but not as we know it *(August 2021)*

"Will you squeeze my avocado?"

I wasn't sure if I heard right.

"Eh? What?" was all I could muster in response.

"I've had an avocado in the 'fridge for a couple of days. I want to see if it is ripe – I've got a plan in mind for dinner tonight if it is" announced Val. "Bruschetta, avocado, and egg topped with a hollandaise sauce. What do you think?"

What I thought was "Has she never heard of a double entendre, it's completely passed her by and come to think of it, it's just as well there weren't two avocados, it would have sounded even worse."

What I said was "Isn't that breakfast?"

"No, that's eggs benedict or is it eggs something else? Whatever... anyway this is..." she stopped and started to giggle. "Oh dear, I've just realised what I've just said."

"What's that? I asked innocently.

"Well I... Oh never mind."

The avocado was ripe so dinner was sorted – except that Val remembered that we had no hollandaise sauce.

"I'll get some in and we'll have it tomorrow."
Sometimes I wonder why I just can't keep my mouth shut.

"Tell you what – I'll make it, can't be that difficult, can it?"

I still don't know why I keep getting it into my head that I am now a competent cook. I get these fits of uncontrollable enthusiasm.

"Well, based on your past performance I'm reserving judgement. It'll keep until tomorrow you know."

I was finding it difficult to understand Val's dubiousness.

Val has a complete library of cookery books, but I am modern man (Hmm..!) so I eschew these books by those such as Oliver, Berry, Smith, Bikers etc. and instead I turned to the internet and printed off a recipe for 'Blender hollandaise sauce' by someone called 'ChellB'. He/she, using a pseudonym, spelt flavour with a 'u' so clearly not American. I can't cope with their cooking measurements, such as 'cup.' As far as I am concerned a cup is for tea and not much else (OK or maybe coffee).

All Present and Correct

The whole thing was simplicity itself. Three egg yolks, a little Dijon mustard, tablespoon of lemon juice and a dash of Tabasco into the blender and blitz for five seconds. 125g of hot melted butter poured in gradually whilst blending at high speed. 'It should thicken immediately' quoted the recipe.

It didn't. It just lay there, totally liquid with a froth on the top, but on the plus side looked the right colour.

I tasted it. "Was it supposed to taste like this?" I wondered. The overriding flavour was a mixture of Dijon and lemon juice. 'ChelleB' said that he/she loved the lemony taste. I was trying to let it not have the opposite effect on me.

Val tasted it. Hopefully she would see something positive. I quote verbatim. "That is the most disgusting thing I have ever tasted in my life. And that includes your previous cookery." She looked at the recipe.

"In every hollandaise sauce recipe I have seen, they used clarified butter, but not so here. That's possibly part of the problem."

"You know, I thought that, but it just said butter so despite my misgivings I followed the instructions" I lied.

This is because I had no idea what clarified butter was. I thought that my ignorance had better be on a 'need to know' basis.

No wonder 'ChelleB' used a pseudonym. How many dinners (or perhaps breakfasts) has he/she ruined? Is this what is known as the dark web? Is no-one safe from malignant individuals with imagined grudges, leaving foul recipes of every description designed to wreck the well meaning amateur cooks' attempts to produce the perfect result?

Or maybe it's just me cooking badly.

Nah! Can't be that.

"I have the hollandaise coming tomorrow with the grocery order so I'll leave it until then" said Val admitting defeat.

"Not a chance!" was my take on it. "I'm going to do a mark II and take the recipe from one of your cookery books." After perusing what seemed like most of the library, I settled on one.

"Look, I have a choice of a classic or simple recipe." I showed her the book.

"Oh please make it the simple one" she sighed. "Only I'm running out of eggs." But she already knew the answer to that.

This recipe called for unsalted butter, and much to my surprise Val produced an 8oz pack. "It was for something I was going to do a while ago and didn't get round to it."
Even more to my surprise when I opened it, it was black. I looked at the sell-by date. It was February.

"Well, actually quite a while ago" she admitted. With my own disaster now disposed of I really wasn't in a position to take the high ground.

"I'll use salted butter and not add salt at a later stage" I decided, now improvising, and as a result feeling quite cheffy.

So, again following the recipe to the letter, I then found out how to clarify butter and also make a sabayon. It is the cooking and thickening of egg yolks whisked until they increase in volume to a cream consistency. See!

Feeding in the butter slowly resulted in something akin to what I was striving for. It certainly tasted way better than my previous effort, in the sense that it tasted of nothing. To the extent that I wondered if somewhere along the line I had contracted Covid-19. Puzzling was the fact that it again was totally liquid.

Liquid Hollandaise

Maybe it was just me feeding in the butter badly.

Nah! Can't be that.

"That's so much better than your last effort. Well done" said Val unconvincingly.

"But it doesn't taste of anything" I countered.
"Exactly" came the reply.

However it was just about good enough for the meal and I wondered if Gary Rhodes would have been happy that I thought his recipe was a cut above that of 'ChelleB.' Anyway - Job done!

The shop bought hollandaise sauce came today and as a matter of interest I looked at the ingredients.

Sunflower oil; water; white wine vinegar; glucose-fructose syrup; free range egg yolk; salt; butter powder (what's that?); modified corn starch; sodium lactate; glucono-delta-lactonel; whey protein concentrate; corn starch; lactic acid; citric acid;

milk proteins; potassium sorbate; lemon juice concentrate; xanthan gum; guar gum; lutien and paprica extract.

So now tell me, with all those ingredients as competition – what chance did I stand?

After Sunday lunch at the Smuggler's Den and a couple of drinks I was feeling particularly mellow as we walked back home through the fields. Maybe it was because of my new found expertise or more likely because of the drink addling my mind, I had this idea...

Farmer Miller Baker *(September 2021)*

1. Farmer

"I come from good honest farming stock you know."

This was my considered opinion, voiced as we walked through one of the three fields back to the village from the pub after Sunday lunch. This year the farmer had planted wheat, and it was now due for harvest.

"I thought you had discovered that you were from a literary background" replied Val.

"Ah! That is on my father's side, but on my mother's side, it is a Cumbrian farming lineage and on her mother's side they were all Dorset agricultural labourers. I definitely have true farming heritage."

"That's Wessex isn't it? Well before you go all Gabriel Oak on me, and start calling me Bathsheba, where are we going with this?"

This was from Thomas Hardy's Wessex based Victorian novel 'Far from the Madding Crowd.' I ignored the comment.

"I want to reclaim my heritage and harvest some wheat. Then I want to make Cornish scones with it. What do you think?"

Val went silent for what I thought was way too long, as the whole idea seemed quite straightforward to me. Eventually however she decided on a response.

"First and foremost, you have a track record on baking" she replied, remembering the bread debacle, but not remembering it was both of us who were responsible. "I don't recall that it ended that well. Secondly, you spent your early working life in a Building Society and the later part as a book dealer. How does that work into reclaiming your farming heritage?"

"Well it doesn't directly fair enough, but walking though this field has brought it home to me. I have to do this to keep the past alive. Also by the way, we made the bread, not just me" I added, scoring a point.

So, a little while later, armed with a carrier bag, and with Val's help, I collected a few sprigs of wheat from the field.

"You asked me to help, but as I am standing here keeping a lookout and definitely not happy, rather than calling it helping, I would call it aiding and abetting. If I get done for this I'll not be pleased."

I suppose technically she was right, so time to talk her round.
"Look, a Waitrose carrier bag (note the green credentials here, a judicious re-use of plastic, but at the same time showing that we are sophisticated) with some stalks in is not going to have any effect at all on a return of wheat in a field that must be over ten acres at least." One look showed that it had little effect on Val either. I tried a different tack and changed the subject. I went back to 'Far from the Madding Crowd'.

"Remember the bit where Sergeant Troy mesmerises Bathsheba by showing off his swordsmanship with a razor sharp blade in a field?" I said. "What if I re-create that? Might be a bit of fun. Would it win you round?"

The response was withering. "You are armed with a pair of scissors. Exactly how are you going to impress me with those? Furthermore, what would your ancestors have thought if they'd seen you bringing the harvest in with a pair of scissors?"

It occurred to me at that point that I might not be doing my agricultural heritage justice.

"Fair enough, OK then let's leg it." I think that's what the seasoned criminal would have said. "I have enough to make a couple of scones."

Ready to Go

Back at home it was time to separate the wheat from the chaff. This turned out to be a lot more difficult than I envisaged. The first test was to see if the wheat was ready. This, according to Google is done by biting into a kernel. If it is soft, then definitely not ready, but if hard it would be OK. I bit on one and it nearly took my tooth out. Clearly ready.

However, I suspected that I had harvested too early, which meant that the wheat stuck to the stalks more that I would have liked, and try as I might, about half stayed exactly where they were when I threshed them. It was almost another week before the farmer combined the field, so clearly I had a lot to learn.

My threshing in order, consisted of brushing the stalks with my fingers, hitting them with a stiff brush, then the end of a rolling pin, stamping on them grape-crushing style, and with half still attached I finally sat for hours in front of the television with a pot on my lap, picking them out by hand for what seemed like weeks.

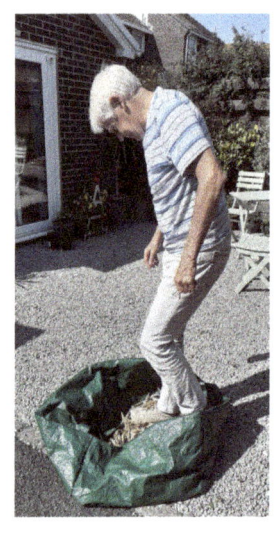

The Various stages of the Threshing

"Can I help?" asked Val, grabbing a pot and some stalks.

"You can, and quite right too. I've danced at your skittish heels, my beautiful Val, for many a long mile, and many a long day; and it is hard to begrudge me this."

"Don't think I don't know what you are doing." She replied. "You are quoting from 'Far From the Madding Crowd' again, aren't you."

"I'm paying homage to my Wessex farming heritage. It's the right thing to do." I said, hoping I'd got the quote right.

"Anyway – what do you mean, skittish?"

I wasn't sure what it meant. I just liked the quote, so I said nothing.

Finally, after a great deal of effort, we had our harvest safely gathered in.

I sat considering the bowl of wheat granules.

Apart from the questionable origin of the wheat... I came to the conclusion that I really could have been a good honest farmer.

2. Miller

Remembering back to when our children were small, I remember times when I would be sitting quietly on my own with the children in another room. I would suddenly be aware that things had actually been very quiet for way too long. Then I would hear "Oh-oh" at which point my heart would sink. Clearly some form of catastrophe would have occurred.

So today, when the quiet was interrupted with "Oh-oh" from the kitchen, followed by "Ray, I need you," The same sinking feeling returned.

On entering the room I was met with a sea of wheat granules spread all over the work surface, the butter dish, behind the bread-bin, all over the floor and probably other places where they will wait to be discovered at regular intervals over the coming years.

"Funny story actually" said Val. "I was just getting something out of the cupboard and knocked the salt pot into the wheat tray". She gave me one of her most engaging smiles, a charming little giggle, and a "Sorry." She continued turning on the charm.

It was the same tactic as she used to employ when we were negotiating book deals, back in the day, and I was always was surprised at how well it worked. Well, I have seen it for over thirty years now and I think I'm immune to it.

So why then, did I spend the next twenty minutes clearing up the mess? Not that I'm OCD but I made sure I found every seed, seeing as I had taken so much trouble to extract every grain from each stalk over the past week. However, at the same time,

I made a mental note to make sure that in the future I would remain immune to her wiles.

I decided that in order to keep the wheat out of harm's way, I would need to start the process of making flour as soon as possible, although it seemed to me that if she was that dangerous with the granules, what mayhem could she cause if she tipped the flour over?
So... how to grind the wheat?

We had a day out on Dartmoor and I had this, what I thought was, a really clever idea, in that I would pick up two large granite blocks, cart them back home and grind the wheat between them, thus replicating the old mills of Victorian times. We were on the old railway track out of Princetown.

We reached just short of Foggintor Quarry, the stone from there was used for Nelson's Column, but now sadly, the quarry was long disused. I spotted two perfect pieces of granite, side by side, just waiting to be used for grinding.

Val agreed. "Perfect" she said. Then... "So why, on a moor awash with granite, did you choose two pieces at the furthest point from the car?"

I really had no answer, and had to put up with her saying nothing about it all the way back to the car, but just waiting for me to wilt under the weight. I was at the same time making out that the stones were not in the slightest bit heavy (which they were).

Back at home, again with the assistance of advice from Google I experimented with putting the wheat in the coffee grinder. Two minutes of action accompanied with the sound of a jet plane landing, meant that surely they must be done. I opened the pot and they they lay there looking exactly as same as when I put them in.

"I hope that hasn't minced the coffee grinder instead" commented Val who was checking to see if a jet plane was landing somewhere close by.

"Bit on the negative side, don't you think" was my response, however carefully checking it. It seemed OK but I hurriedly put it away just in case.

I tried a mortar and pestle. Again, no effect whatsoever.

So, now what I was hoping for all along. The Dartmoor stones. I was looking forward to this. To get the lower stone flat, which it had to be, I had to balance it on pieces of wood. I put some seeds on top as a test, and then used the smaller stone to grind the seeds down.

This really was recreating the ways of times past. From being a farmer, I now pictured myself being in charge of a Victorian milling operation, wheat arriving at one end of the mill, the millstones doing their thing, and bags of flour being loaded on to horse-drawn carriages at the other end.

The daydream ended as quickly as it started as I examined the result. I was successful with a few seeds. The rest just rolled away.

"How are you doing?" asked Val, also examining the result.

"Not going as well as I'd hoped" I replied.

Somehow I think she had realised long before I had, that it could not possibly work and that the whole idea had been bordering insane. The stones are now an attractive feature in the garden, but every time I look at them I remember the pain of carrying them back to the car.

So, what to do next?

I just tipped a load of seeds into the blender.

This immediately brought Val rushing back into the kitchen to check on the situation regarding jet planes, as the noise was deafening. But...seconds later we had flour!

Sieving the "blended" wheat Flour ... and the leftovers

"I knew this would work" I said in a very positive manner.

"And I believe you" replied Val, not believing me.

I put the result though a fine sieve, re-blended the remains of the first batch about four times, and repeated the operation for the rest of the seeds.

I sat considering the carton of finely graded flour.

I came to the conclusion that I really could have been a good honest miller.

3. Baker

With the harvesting and milling now complete, it was time to do something with the flour. I was looking for a good quality recipe, once again on Google. Actually, what did we do before search engines were invented? We have 102 cook books in our library (yes Val, I've counted them) but it is so much easier to use the computer.

I found one with using plain flour, salt, caster sugar, baking powder, lard, butter and milk, with egg and milk for the egg wash.
I was a bit perturbed by the fact that they called it a Devonshire cream tea, but on the other hand, satisfactorily, the picture showed the jam on first, so it must have been Cornish. They also used Chantilly cream for the topping. Well, of course that cannot be. No self respecting cream tea uses anything else but clotted cream, wherever it comes from. My concern was that the rest of the recipe might have also been that inaccurate.

Now given my track record so far on almost everything I have touched in the kitchen (Seasalt, crisps, cheese, soup – sorry bisque, cauliflower puree, bread and the like) I have to say I was not confident of producing anything eatable, although I really did think that I was rapidly improving. Val actually disappeared upstairs, I suspected because she couldn't watch. I was happy about that.

I once employed a builder to do some work for me and at the same time, in the same room, I put up some shelves. Every few minutes I realised he was watching what I was doing, saying nothing, but at the same time saying so much silently. It was one of the most unnerving experiences of my life. If Val had stayed to watch I would have had the same experience for sure.

Anyway, I just chucked everything into a bowl, mixed it by hand, added milk, put it on a tray in eleven round blobs (the recipe said twelve but I guessed the size and got it wrong) and shoved the lot in the oven for ten minutes. It actually took fifteen.

Val reappeared. I took the small scone (there is always the leftover bit) broke it in half and we tasted it.

Silence. Then... the verdict from the master.
Success !

"My goodness, that really does taste nice. Perfectly cooked, a certain crispness on the outside and soft in the middle" was her take on it.

"A triumph!" Although she didn't actually say that bit, surely she must have thought it, and if she didn't, I did! Nothing at all had gone wrong.

Well, 3 pm. and time to eat. I laid it all out as perfectly as I could and was ready to go. I sat considering the cream tea.

I came the the conclusion that I really could have been a good honest baker.

Cream tea for two

Post Script: Would I do it again? Not a cat's chance in hell!

Now that all restrictions were lifted the grand-children could come and visit...

Newspaper Wars *(October 2021)*

Cornish Guardian vs. Newquay Voice. So which is better? We've just unwillingly taken part in the ultimate test.

Grand-daughter announces on her way back to home in Exeter that she is about to be sick. Val grabbed our new copy of the CG, cupped it and caught the first load. We stopped the car.

Second event (and there always is one!) the also unread NV came to hand. This was also effective but to be fair there was less the second time.

I have to report that the CG came up trumps and nothing soaked through it. The NV is thinner but also did the job. We pronounced it a draw as we decided that we did not wish to examine either too closely. Thanks to Hannah and Val for carrying out this experiment.

Anyone know a good car valet?

It was months since we had been allowed visit to relatives up country, but now it gave us a chance to be sightseers as well...

Handel vs. Dylan *(October 2021)*

We were in the Bate Collection of Musical Instruments in Oxford. More than 1000 instruments are on display by the most important English, French and German makers, according to the blurb.

It seemed to me from what I saw, that we were actually allowed to play them, but just to be sure I checked with the Curator.

"Oh yes" he said. "This is a primary research facility for students of the Faculty of Music and visiting researchers. Student are in here regularly testing them out."

"Magic" I thought, and Val and I had a great time experimenting with all sorts of instruments.

The Forbidden Harpsichord

I saw a harpsichord. This really interested me, never having played one before – come to think of it I don't think I had even seen one close up, so it was a golden opportunity. I sat down and bashed out a tune, (very poorly, I can only play a couple of tunes).

The curator came flying up to me.

"What are you doing" he gasped.

"I thought I'd test out the harpsichord as it looked so interesting."

He held his head.

"That harpsichord was owned by George Frederick Handel. He composed some of his greatest works on it. It's there for display purposes only and you are not allowed to touch it."

In my defence there was no sign on it to say so that I could see.

"So I'd rather you didn't" he added, in a voice which was so polite, and at the same time so menacing.

On the way out I thought about it.

"Val – there is a harpsichord in Oxford that has had Handel's 'Messiah' composed on it, and Bob Dylan's 'Mr Tambourine Man' played on it. Surely that has to be a world's first."

"You must be so proud" said Val.

Masks were still the order of the day at the time when we took our first holiday for a couple of years.

Frith vs. Frith *(October 2021)*

The Hell Bay Hotel "Golf Course"

I have only ever played one round of golf. This was back in the 1980's when I was invited, by my friend Steve who sadly is now no longer with us, to join him and a couple of other friends at Truro Golf Club to play the 18 hole course.

As we were progressing around the course, he stopped and considered my technique.

"Interesting. I see you are using the motor-boat method of play" he remarked.

"I thought I would" I replied, having no idea what he was talking about. "...um... exactly what do you mean?"

"Putt, putt, putt, all the way" was his rejoinder, which caused much amusement to the rest of the party.

To be fair, although most of my shots went in the general direction of the hole, very few, if any, actually left the ground.

Then and there I decided that golf would not be the game for me.

There is a golf course at the Hell Bay Hotel on Bryher. Val and I have a tradition that we always play one game on it, the winner claiming the bragging rights, which can last sometimes for a couple of years until our next visit.

Now, the Royal and Ancient it isn't. The main differences are: 1. There are only five holes. 2. None are over 100 yards long. 3. There are no greens. 4. There are no fairways. In fact it is just a field with five battered tees and five holes with equally battered foot high flags.

Nevertheless, as we were on the island this week it was absolutely essential that I won the bragging rights back after several years of putting up with the description of what happened the last time we played. Neither of us remember the result, as it was totally eclipsed by Val's shot on the 4th. She shaped up, hit the ball and we watched it form a perfect arc, and land an inch from the hole, where it stopped dead. It was the perfect shot, and every time Bryher is mentioned the tale is regaled. I'd have done the same if it was me – but it wasn't!

The clubs are kept in a store beside the first tee, so firstly we asked at reception for a couple of balls. The receptionist was wearing the obligatory mask, and handed us not one, but two balls each. I couldn't see, but I was sure she was smiling knowingly.

"Well I thought she was as well" agreed Val, but neither of us could think why.

In the store there were a myriad of clubs and putters, but as always I had to dig down for ages to find a left handed club or putter. In the end I found the only two there. One of these days I will do a piece on the rampant anti-leftism that persists in Britain to this day – but OK, that's for another time.

We made our own local rule that, as the field had rabbits who seemed to think the best place for a hole was between tee and flag only to think better of it and leave golf ball sized holes, we would allow a free dropped ball if it landed in one of the holes.

I think it fair to say that the first hole was a disaster. I found that I could still not get the ball off the ground, whilst Val managed, first shot, to move the ball about two feet. In all we drew the 1st 10 -10. I put it down to just needing to get our eye in.

Hole two was better, however there was an intense discussion, with a full and frank exchange of views, as to whether air shots counted as a stroke or not. I still think they should, but unaccountably, although the final vote was 1-1, I was in fact outvoted.

At hole three I realised that I probably had demonstrated Sir Isaac Newton's First Law of Motion successfully. Maybe it could be used as an example in lectures on the subject. An object at rest remains at rest, and an object in motion remains in motion at constant speed and in a straight line unless acted on by an unbalanced force.

The ball did not at all move in a straight line, because I was the "unbalanced force" acting upon it. It flew almost sideways and disappeared into the undergrowth, unfortunately never to re-appear. Another full and frank exchange of views followed resulting in confirmation that a dropped ball cost me another stroke.

Hole four was the scene of Val's triumph last time. Not so here. She gave it some 'wellie' fair enough, but this time it flew straight into the hedge, also never to appear again.

Game On!

"I think a dropped ball counts as a stroke, as you'll remember we agreed" I said as casually as possible.

The final hole was really no better than the rest. We were actually the only ones out there and this was probably just as well, as we holed out, both of us, by zig-zagging our way so widely that Val was back on the second with her second shot, and I was on the third with my third. Ha! Symmetry in action.

The road to the hotel runs along the ridge at the top of the field. We realised that there were walkers out for a stroll. "Don't worry – we weren't watching" one of them called out. Satisfied that we believed them they went on their way.

"Of course they were watching us, we were playing so badly" Val muttered. "I would have been."

We handed back the remaining to balls to the masked receptionist.

"Sorry" said Val, "but we lost a couple." That was the reason for the knowing smile under the mask. She had clearly known from the start that we would not come back with the same number we started with.

"Don't worry, it's quite usual" she said. "Did you have a good game?"

"Really good fun" we replied in unison, trying to believe it ourselves and our differences almost, but not quite forgotten.

The result and bragging rights, at the end of the day don't really matter of course, we really did have a good time and we love having these little traditions to look back on over the years...

...and who am I trying to kid!

Of course it matters - especially as this time they are all mine, so the score sheet says...Sorry Val, but this time you got toasted.

The Final Tally

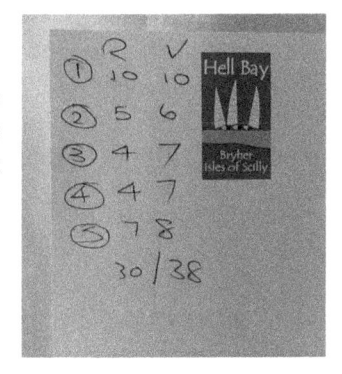

Hopefully this Christmas would be a sight better than last year now that we were free again, but some things never change unfortunately...

Black Friday *(November 2021)*

Remember - it's Black Friday today.

So, time for action. Debit and credit cards, cheque book (remember them?) and cash all to be safely tucked away, and absolutely nothing to be bought today - not even a newspaper.

If everybody in the country did the same this obnoxious import of greed and manic consumerism from America could be packed up and sent back where it came from.

Ah well! One can only dream...

Facebook comment from Valerie: "I have a confession to make Ray. I've just bought a lottery ticket."

My reply: "I am a person of principle Valerie, consequently I will have absolutely nothing to do with any winnings at all on a ticket bought today!"

"Oh!...er...hang on a minute, let me think this through..."

I wanted to put my cooking skills to a new test. Christmas was not far away so I thought I would help by making something we would normally buy...

Crisps *(November 2021)*

"It's about time I did some cooking for Christmas" I announced "...and I want to do something that we wouldn't normally have during the year." Clearly I had thought this through and was going to make a declaration.

Val looked up, with the mention of cooking catching her interest immediately.

"Crisps" I said.

"Crisps" she echoed slowly. I felt that as suddenly as it came, her interest was disappearing.

"Of all the things you could have come up with, you chose crisps? So far you've made butter, wrecking the kitchen, you made sea-salt, turning it into a mini sauna and I hesitate to even mention the cauliflower puree debacle. Why can't you make something conventional?"

"Where's the fun in that?" was my only thought, however I refused to be deflated.

"Look – we never buy them except at Christmas, they have to be simple to make, and you'll surely change your mind when you are snacking on them on Christmas Day."

The reason I chose crisps was that about five years ago, Val was wandering through Lidl's and bought a mandolin, falling into their dastardly centre isle trap where they lure you into a fit of impulse buying. There it remained in the cupboard, still in its box, untouched and unloved.

Until of course today! I was determined to cook something using it, and the only thing I could think of was crisps. So with four potatoes, salt, cider vinegar and olive oil, I was ready to rumble. I use that word to show how my enthusiasm had taken hold.

That is until I took the mandolin out of the box. No instructions and about twelve pieces. I spotted some notes on the box. It said "Einsatzehalter Die – und Streifeneinsatze werden eingeschnappt" to start with. "One of the drawbacks of using Lidl they don't tell you about" I thought. "OK so down to me on my own then."

First thing to do of course was to pour a glass of wine. This is an essential first step in any cookery endeavour (Examples: Graham Kerr, Keith Floyd etc. for those of a certain age).

It took ten minutes to work out the minutiae of the contraption, but finally I was slicing away, and if I do say so myself, the potential crisps were looking exactly how they should. I soaked them in cider vinegar and sea salt for twenty minutes and then coated them with the olive oil and more salt, finally laying them on trays ready for the oven. In they went for around half an hour, but to be checked after fifteen minutes.

"This kitchen smells awful" was Val's first comment. I hadn't realised how potent cider vinegar was, and she was right. It reeked.

Then "Whilst you were doing whatever...I've book us a holiday." Clearly she was doing something more useful than I was.

"This is turning into a really productive day" I opined to myself. Holiday and crisps! Happiness was everywhere as I sat down to arrange the travel insurance. Not so straightforward and it took time, but eventually – all sorted.

Of course when you are at the top, the only way is downwards.

Val's second comment was the similar to the first. "What's that smell from the kitchen?" was of all the things Val could say probably was the one that gave me the biggest sinking feeling possible.

The Burnt Crisps

I dived for the oven way too late and there they were, perfectly shaped crisps – and perfectly black.

I think it a well known fact that at such a point the worst thing to do is to ask pointless questions. A sample from Val were...

"Did you forget them?" This was a phrase which is something akin to the one where, when you have lost something, they say "well where did you last have it?" only marginally more annoying.

Why didn't you put the timer on?" and "I've just bought the cider vinegar – did you use it all?" are equally annoying.

"...and did you get the travel insurance?" was one that particularly stuck in my mind.

Most annoying of all though was "Oh by the way, I forgot to tell you – I had already bought crisps as part of our Christmas order."

Being back to normality the newspapers still had the ability to wind me up – although probably it was just as much because of my age...

Sulfur *(November 2021)*

Please consider the word above.

First and foremost I would imagine you are wincing at the perceived mis-spelling, and that the correct spelling is Sulphur.

However I would imagine you would then go on to assume it to be a chemical element, quite probably last used in earnest when you were at school. Some, who are more into the sciences, may be able to go further and say that it has the chemical element symbol 'S', is bright yellow and is solid at room temperature.

Finally you may realise that, apart from in pub quizzes, you will probably not ever need to use the word again.

Anyway, today I read in the newspapers that Sulfur is now the correct spelling.

There is a quisling in the ranks of The Royal Society of Chemistry collaborating with the enemy forces now at war with us, who are subversively trying to overturn the Queen's English and impose the vastly inferior American version.

This is the argument used...

It has 'decided' that 'to avoid confusion' all UK textbooks and examination papers should henceforth adopt what is thought of by dictionary scholars in the UK to be the American spelling, viz. sulfur. Recently the same diktat also came from QCA, the regulatory authority for examinations in England, a diktat forwarded to those who have been involved in writing the new A-level syllabuses.

Is it seriously possible that they think that anyone at all could be confused by the the word sulphur?

Surely, anyone who is, should not be allowed anywhere near a chemistry laboratory as they'd be a danger to themselves and everyone around them. Who knows what chemicals they could confuse! But unfortunately a Royal Society no less, has turned traitor on Britain and now the American spelling it is then.

The insidious advance of American English has to be stopped.

We shall fight them in Dictionaries. We shall fight them in Thesauruses, (or is it Thesaurai?) we must... Sorry – getting a little carried away there.

We were on a three hour ferry ride to the Isles of Scilly, and I was reading every last word in the newspaper to pass the time, and I came upon that article which touched a language nerve. (Don't get me started on the listings there... "shopping cart; gotten; expiration and the like... and my biggest bugbear – 24/7 followed by the pause so you can admire their clever way with words, when they could just say "all the time")

Hold on though. Perhaps all is not lost. We were booked into an exqusitely British hotel. Fair enough is is on the Isles of Scilly, and about as far a possible as one can get away from this insanity.

Everything there from the paintings on the walls, all orginals, to the food on the plates remains resolutely British. It may be the last bastion of our heritage, so we wallowed in it's homeliness.

But wait!

I was perusing the menu for the evening meal, delighting in the locally produced food, which was, just as it should have been, classily British.

And then I saw it. There on the list of ingredients for a couple of the dishes. I looked again, and it really was there...

"Slaw."

Even these walls are crumbling – there is no hope.

The Intruder

It appears we have had an intruder in the house – and it is not for the first time. I have never seen this person and I cannot see how he/she has got in – but he/she undoubtedly has managed it. Strangely, all he/she does is hide things, and sometimes makes things, usually of little or no value, disappear completely. Always unseen he/she moves around the house and causes Val great difficulty – she has even given him/her a name. It's "someone."

This morning she found that "someone" had moved a card she had cut out, and had put it in the bin. Yesterday "someone" had moved the scissors. She has begun to think that as he/she is here so often that he/she should do things to help.

"Someone" has not washed up properly she said to me recently, although I cannot honestly see how she could expect him/her to do domestic chores.

I denied moving something last week. "Well someone has" she replied instantly.

Has anyone else had this problem with intruders?

~~~~~

Random Facebook posts: Quote of the morning by someone who shall remain nameless.... "I was not nagging, I was just explaining what you had done wrong!"

Another quote from someone who, again will remain nameless.

"I'm not blaming you, I'm just pointing out that you did it".

I did not have a reply.

Over the past eighteen months or so my cooking prowess had progressed by leaps and bounds/had not improved in the slightest and if anything was getting worse. You chose one of those two depending which one of us you were speaking to.

Soda Bread *(November 2021)*

We knew we were living above our station in life at the hotel on Bryher, when we were presented with a range of different breads to accompany our evening meals. Still, that's what holidays are all about.

This included soda bread. I had not had this before and it really tasted delightful – to the extent that Val decided that we must have some when we got home. I agreed, but in reality thought no more about it.

In last week's grocery order, two bags of Duchy Organic Stoneground Strong Bread Flour appeared, one wholemeal, one white. They were from Waitrose – we were still trying to live the high life as we had got used to it after a week on the island, but they were half price for some reason, so it was OK.

"I see you are wanting me to make some soda bread then" I stated remembering our conversation.

"Oh that...er.. not exactly" replied Val. "No thank you – I would like some nice bread."

"Bit harsh" I thought, taken aback.

"No – I'm going to have a go myself and make ordinary bread. We'll buy the soda bread." Val was remembering my last disastrous effort to make bread, it wasn't good. I was on the back foot again. Surely she was aware of my progress as a chef since that time, and anyway I still thought it was both of us making the bread last time.

"Look, if you want Soda Bread I'll get it from the bakery counter at the supermarket" was the response. So perhaps not then.

"Well OK, I'm ready and waiting if you change your mind."

"No. Happy to buy it." She seemed adamant.

Well apparently Sainsburys, Morrisons and even Waitrose do not make their own Soda Bread. They just supply it on the shelves wrapped in plastic.

"It's a no go I'm afraid" said Val in a very disappointed manner. "None of them do it themselves, can't think why not."

It had the opposite effect on me. "Right then, baking it is, because I can." My enthusiasm was burgeoning.

"No – it's OK, I should have tried the local baker in the village. Why didn't I think of that before?" and with that she was off to sort the matter out, only to return ten minutes later, crestfallen.

"Apparently, there is no call for it and they've stopped making it. It's got such a great taste, I can't think why it's not more popular" she continued resignedly. I think she was bowing to the inevitable.

"I saw my chance. Not to worry – I've got this. I know exactly what to do. You want Soda Bread, and you shall have some!"

I couldn't understand why she wasn't displaying the same enthusiasm as I was.

"Really?" she said disinterestedly.

Actually I hadn't got a clue what to do, but I regarded that information to be on a "need to know" basis, and Val didn't need to know. So some research on Google seemed to be the order of the day – actually when Val wasn't looking.

"You know I'm a quarter Irish" I said. "This is on my father's side, so this time I'm going to reclaim my literary Irish heritage. One of my ancestors was a published author. I'm going to make Irish Soda Bread!"

There was silence.

Then... "There is no way you know about Irish Soda Bread without having checked it on Google. No way at all." Well, she was not wrong there.

"I need wholemeal flour, plain flour, buttermilk, bicarbonate of soda, and salt." I announced, "...and I've just realised that I have made wholemeal flour, salt and buttermilk before, so I could make them all again." Perhaps I was going over the top.

"You are out of season for the wheat, you'd have to buy pints of cream for the buttermilk, and last time you made salt, the kitchen was damp for days afterwards." She was right of course. That's the trouble with Val, way too much common sense.

We were in Sainsbury's looking at a large range of different flour packets.

"I think what you will need is some sort of strong bread flour" said Val in one of those voices tinged with authority.

"Ah! No. Sorry but the recipe says plain flour, and I have to follow it to the letter. In fact I am AC/DC about that." I too could put on the voice.

"Well I don't see how it will rise" she replied "...and...er... did you say that right? I think you have said that you are..."

Oops! Obsessive/compulsive is what I meant." I interrupted. "Actually, what does..."

"Never Mind." Val's turn to interrupt. " I think you are going to have trouble with this – it'll turn out to be a doorstop."

Finding the buttermilk was easier than I thought, I grabbed a couple of pots and armed with all the necessary, I was ready to go.

Val was going away for a couple of days. "You could make it while I'm away – it'll give you something to do" she said. "And perhaps having eaten it by the time I get back?" Was she joking, or was she serious? Her lack of enthusiasm had not gone unnoticed.

"Sorry, I've got to do it today" was my response. "The buttermilk 'use by' date is today, so best if I get on with it."

"You've done it again haven't you. I mean, what were you thinking!"

Again she was right. In my haste and my eagerness I had broken the golden rule of shopping. Always go to the furthest from the front and pick the item with the longest sell/use by date from the back. I had just grabbed the front carton, so today had to be the big day. Val had gone out, so time to get it all ready for her return.

Enough Flour to Sink a Battleship but the Waitrose organic is out of bounds.

It actually couldn't be simpler. Just weigh out and chuck all the dry stuff in a bowl, mix, add the buttermilk, a quick knead and all done. Baking tray for half an hour, and hey presto!

Halfway though the wait however, I lost confidence and as I had some more buttermilk I made another using a different recipe, this time adding rosemary and honey.

As predicted, the first came out looking and feeling just like a doorstop. Gloom descended as I looked at the second, which to be honest appeared overcooked. I laid them out side by side ready for inspection.

On Val's return we had a ceremonial tasting event. First, the touch test. Both had the weight and the feel of a doorstop. I cut into the first. To my surprise, apart from the crust which was hard, totally soft in the middle. All talk of a doorstop assuaged as we tasted it.

"Are you transported back to the Hell Bay Hotel?"

"Actually – yes I am" was the reply. "It tastes exactly the same. Really Good."

On a high, I cut into the second.

"Burnt on the outside, and look – not cooked at all in the middle" was Val's take on it. Clearly the oven had been too hot for that one. "Tastes a bit sickly too." That must have been the honey.

Before and After!

Well for every high there must be a low, and for every wave caught there must be a wipe out I suppose. The second loaf was consigned to the bin.

"I wonder why it is called Irish?" queried Val.

"I think it was as a result of the famine – it was simple, few ingredients and was used as a main meal." I had done some studying. "In the north they cut it into four triangles but in the south, they cut a cross in the dough and prepare copious amounts for St Patrick's Day. I have ancestors from Ofally so I'm with the cross."

"I feel that I have now done my Irish heritage justice. "However we must not, under any circumstances make any more."

"Why not?" Val was puzzled.

"The unique texture of soda bread is a result of the reaction between the acidic sour milk and baking soda, which forms small bubbles of carbon dioxide in the dough." I replied.

"That's right – on the very day that COP 26 is trying to decide how to limit global warming, I have just increased our carbon footprint by two soda breads worth."

There was only one thing to do.

"We are helping ruin the planet. I'm off to telephone the grandchildren to apologise!"

December and for the few of us who don't regard the run up to Christmas should start before then, it was time to get cracking...

Christmas *(December 2021)*

Val has bought a Christmas Tree! Setting aside the fact that we already have one, and I suppose you can never have too many of course - it came with instructions. Apparently we must not eat it.

To all intents and purposes life was back to normal, although as still in the vulnerable category we should still be taking care...

Parking *(February 2022)*

Yesterday I was driving into Morrison's Car Park. I chose my parking space and was halfway in when...

"That looks a good space over there."

"But I'm already in here" I replied.

"It's miles away from the entrance."

This was true. I have always parked away from the doors of the supermarket because I always worry about others banging their doors against our car when they get out. At the back I choose a space where there is no-one parking either side.

"But it doesn't work anyway."

Val was right. It doesn't. Wherever I park, and however much I am far away from anyone else, by the time we come out someone parks right next to me. I've never understood why that happens.

However, this is not an unusual scenario. I always receive parking advice, whether the car park be empty, half full or just two spaces left. Quite often Val does spot a much better space. I can't, of course admit this, and continue with my own choice, and at the same time trying to think of some coherent reason why I had parked where I did, that she would actually believe.

Sometimes there is only one space left. Then...

"Are you sure you've parked it straight?" or "I think you are over the line this side."
I admit that on the odd occasion I just reply airily "Oh that'll be fine" and we go on our way with me hoping inside that being slightly over the line doesn't result in me getting a ticket. The fine would be incidental to the comments I would get from Val if I did, which do not bear thinking about.

However, back to yesterday. This is a regular trip so I am now used to the comments I get each time, such as:

"That's fine. I think I can almost see Morrison's from here" or

"I wonder if we should call a taxi."

...but her latest today was: "Do they offer a park and ride here?"

Onwards and upwards as they say. Surely any chef in Cornwall must be able to make a Cornish Pasty. As I now considered myself to be one, it was time for me to master this technique, it being brought home to me by a television programme.

The Cornish Pasty *(February 2022)*

I was watching Rick Stein's series on Cornwall and he was eulogising over the one and only correct way to make a Cornish Pasty. Apparently these days all manner of ingredients are deigned to be acceptable as constituent parts. Steak, tomatoes and even carrots are regularly used and there is such a thing as a cheese and onion pasty, which surely is a contradiction in terms.

"I think I ought to fly the flag for my Cornish heritage and make a genuine Cornish pasty" I announced to Val as the programme ended.

She was looking at me quizzically.

"What Cornish heritage is that then?" she queried. "Your mother came from a long line of English agricultural labourers and your father was mostly Irish." I would have preferred it if she had called them farmers, although in reality it might have been stretching the point.

"Well, I've lived in Cornwall for forty-three years, I have a Cornish son, born in Treliske, went to Goonhavern and Tretherras schools and he has a St. Piran flag sticker on the bumper of his car – and you don't get more Cornish than that" I replied emphatically.

I ignored the fact that my two other sons are 'Men of Kent' (not 'Kentish Men', who are born the wrong side of the River Medway) and my only Cornish son now lives in Warwickshire.

All too late. I was on the case now, and a quick look at Google supplied me with a recipe although puzzlingly it was titled "Rick Stein Cornish Pasty Recipe Crescent."

"Bit weird" I thought but printed it off anyway.

Val was going to Morrison's to do the shopping whilst I was at training, the price being that I had to buy her a Sports Centre breakfast when she came to pick me up.

"I need beef skirt, swede..."

"You mean turnips don't you – you won't get far if you call them swedes in Cornwall."

I didn't think this was the time to discuss the technical differences between the two – apparently there are some and they could be called, just as correctly, rutabagas, or in Cornish - routabagys. I kid you not.

I continued "...and clotted cream." I finished the list.

There was silence.

"Clotted Cream?" She eventually repeated. "Are you sure you have got the recipe right – there surely is no way clotted cream is any part of a traditional Cornish Pasty."

I showed her my printed list. It had Rick Stein's picture at the top, and there it was...

"6 heaped teaspoons of clotted cream or butter."

Val disappeared, but I distinctly heard muttering as she went.

The ingredients and the suspect recipe

So here I was ready to go. I laid out all the ingredients on the table. First problem was that the beef skirt was only 300g as opposed to the recipe which was 450g.

"There's not enough beef skirt" I commented.

"You never said how much you wanted" replied Val. This was accompanied by the cold stare. I decided then and there that of course it was enough and I'd reduce the whole recipe by 33%. I looked at the recipe for the pastry and it read (word for word)...

"Using the tips of the fingers or having a table knife, chop within the flour using the butter before the flour continues to be added to the butter. The protuberances of butter and flour could be still quite big. Pour within the chilled water a little at any given time..."

At that point I gave up – the recipe did not make any sense at all and I really was having some difficulty regarding it's authenticity.

I just took a roll of ready made shortcrust pastry out of the 'fridge and scrapped that part of the procedure. I know it's cheating a bit but I've seen chefs do it on screen so it must be OK.

Luckily, I know what a pasty should look like, so I just diced all the ingredients, chopped the beef skirt into small strips and put them into three piles.

So to continue with the recipe...

"Unveil the pastry – not very thinly. Cut disc shapes about 25cm – supper plate size – across. Convey a ball of filling on every disc of pastry and draft two edges to create a half-moon shape and crimp the perimeters together."

That sort of made sense, and ten minutes later I had something that actually looked like pasties. I was supposed to put a teaspoon of butter on the top of each one, but I decided that in deference to the recipe, in the third one I put a teaspoon of clotted cream instead.

Now the crimping – and back to the recipe...

"Moisten the advantage from the pastry, contain the edges from you, roll the pastry together with your right forefront finger upon your left thumb and forefront finger – it's some art so just operate a fork within edges."

Best ignore all that I thought and just used the back of a teaspoon.

Done, egg washed, and into the oven on greased trays for around an hour or so.

I had time now so I decided to investigate this recipe properly and there on the list was Ингредиенты. (Ingredients).

Russian!

I discovered that Rick Stein's recipe had been translated into Russian and then translated back again, I suspect by a computer. I now knew the meaning of the phrase "Lost in Translation."

Was the aggressive expansionist regime of President Putin extending to attacking our precious Cornish pasty recipes? Was the clotted cream placed in the recipe as some sort of I E D ready to sabotage the whole operation? Was I in some way supporting Putin's world domination objective by following the recipe?

Hopefully not – but it was time for the taste test.

The finished article

We had pasty and beans for dinner and it looked, tasted and smelt like a traditional Cornish pasty. Job done I thought.

However, the clotted cream version is now in the freezer, ready for another day.

Well you can't have too much excitement all at once, can you?

Shopping *(March 2022)*

I was tasked with doing the shopping whilst Val was away – but no problem of course as she had left me a list. On it was Andrex toilet rolls – again no problem, or so I thought.

Let me run through the choice available. 'Gentle Clean'; 'Skin Kind'; 'Shea Butter' (really!); 'Quilts'; 'Classic Clean' and get the – 'Natural pebble'. There was no further information on my list.

The Andrex Range in Morrisons

So, would I prefer 'Classic Clean'? But then 'Gentle Clean' sounded better, although 'Skin Kind' might be ideal.

Where did these names come from? Someone high up in Andrex presumably tested the various versions and I suddenly had the horrendous picture of a panel testing out each armed with a pen and note pad eulogising over the benefits of 'Classic Clean' as opposed to say 'Skin Kind' as they sat on the loo.

I'm sure that Andrex have done their market reseach, but if you look at the range objectively – are they not all insane? It's just toilet paper.

But all the did not solve my immediate problem of which would be the most beneficial, and crucially – which would cause the least recriminations when Val returned.

In the end I spotted one on the end of the aisle which was labelled 'Aloe Vera'.

No idea what it means but I like to live dangerously.

As far as I was concerned there was by now no cookery challenge that was too great for me. If the supermarket had run out of something – I would just make it instead!

Croissants *(April 2022)*

Where are the best croissants to be found? Well, in my humble, totally biased and uninformed opinion they are 39p each from Lidl. But there is a problem. Why do they always have chocolate croissants available but so often there are no butter variety available? You'd think if there was a shortage, the flavoured variety would be put on the skids. Well, not so!

I decided to rebel. Starved of my normal breakfast fayre I decided to make my own. Seemed to be quite simple according to Val.

"All you need is a roll of puff pastry cut it, roll it into a croissant shape, and bake it." was her take on it.

I was not so sure, but I was really annoyed with Lidl for not having any in stock this morning so I was really up for it. I purloined the one roll of "Jus-Rol" puff pastry from the freezer, let it thaw and off I went.

I decided to use the counter top as the base as I didn't think any of the chopping boards would be large enough, and deftly and carefully unrolled the pastry. I peeled off the greaseproof paper and suddenly realised something. I had forgotten to flour the counter, this resulted in the dough being stuck fast.

Now, usually at this point Val would normally appear, having some sort of radar which tells her when I've made my latest 'faux pas'.

I looked at the door. There was no-one there.

"Result" I thought.

I found it was incredibly difficult to extract it, although it was finally achieved with the aid of a scraper. Counter now suitably floured I started again. Now misshapen due to my efforts, I rolled out the pastry to make it larger, cut it into six triangles and rolled them into shape.

They looked like croissants!

"Don't forget to egg wash them" came a voice from the other room.

Val knew what I was doing! So, was she aware of my sticky pastry problem? Anyway I cracked an egg.

"Make sure you use one of the small eggs – you don't need to use much."

"Now she tells me" I thought and decided to keep quiet about the fact that I had chosen a large one, or to be more correct I just happened to grab the first egg I saw which was large. I beat the egg ready for the procedure.

"Don't forget to separate the yoke." I heard next.

"Bit late now" was my only thought. That really was to only be disclosed on a need to know basis, so I kept quiet about that as well.

I egg washed the croissants and tipped the rest of the egg away.

"Tell you what, I'll have scrambled egg for lunch so can you save it for me."

This was surreal. Was I caught is some sort of time warp where my life had been jolted out of sync. with the rest of the world? Maybe it was Val who had entered a parallel universe. Who knew how this would end.

Our worlds came crashing back together when she appeared at the door.

"They're a bit small – with that amount of pastry you should only cut four out." I had done six. "...and they look a bit thin."

"Oh that happened when I rolled the pastry out" I replied.

Silence.

"Sorry, did you say you rolled the puff-pastry out?"

She repeated it. "You rolled the puff-pastry out?"

I had this sinking feeling. I had this sudden realisation that what I had done might just have been more than a little daft.

"Guess what happens if you roll out puff-pastry."

"Um... I guess that it rolls out all the puff?" I muttered somewhat sheepishly.

She beamed.

"All you had to do was unroll it, cut it into four and cook it. How on earth could you get that wrong? I mean, what were you thinking!"

A point well made I thought.

I looked at the packet. "DO NOT USE A ROLLING PIN" it said in capitals, as if taunting me.

Oven on at 200 and in for 12 minutes. Checked at 15 minutes and again at 17 minutes. At 20 minutes I (or rather Val) considered them done.

I have say, although rather flat, rather small and not in the least buttery, (see illustration: Frith version vs. real version) they tasted OK.

...but I so do hope Lidl re-stock soon, I can't go through all that again.

Croissants: Frith version vs. Real Version

The fact that I now considered myself an expert chef did not deter Val from giving me what she called "helpful advice." I was not normally asked if I wanted it or not though...

The Look *(June 2022)*

I got the look again this morning.

Before I go any further I perhaps ought to go into a bit of history.

Many years ago I was a District Manager in a company called "Woolwich Building Society." I had, of course been promoted one step above my competence level, as was usual in those days. I think they call it "The Peter Principle" now. This meant that I was always fighting a rear guard action, trying to bluff my way through the various crises caused mainly by myself.

I had an assistant/secretary, a lovely middle-aged lady, not old enough to be my mother's age – but not far off. She had been there for years and knew all there was to know about everything. She always got on with whatever I gave her to do, and really was the perfect partner to my incompetence. Her name was Marge and whatever I did she never commented.

However...

If I asked her to do something which in her opinion was wrong, all she did was allow her glasses to slip slightly down her nose and just looked at me over them.

"...er...although, of course, alternatively we could do it this way" I would stammer and shuffle my feet uncertainly until she looked away, satisfied that she had corrected matters. It was like a death ray. In my mind it pinned me against the wall ready for the oncoming firing squad. If scientists could capture it in some physical form, it would be the ultimate improvement of the laser. The "Look of Marge" was the enduring memory of my days there.

I had never seen before, anyone else who could strike someone down with just a look, but sometime last week...

I had decided that I was overcomplicating my cooking and I was going to try making shortbread biscuits. Just three ingredients: butter, sugar and flour – what could possibly go wrong.

In fact I said "Look – leave it to me, I know what I am doing!" to Val after she had given me some helpful hints.

Her glasses slipped down her nose and she just stared at me over them.

It was the "Look of Marge!"

"...er...well perhaps I could do with some advice." I found that I had said that almost before I had even realised she was looking at me.

There followed all sorts of instructions as to how the perfect shortbread should be made, and to be fair, the finished result was really tasty.

But I was now curious as to how the 'Look of Marge' had transported itself over the years and between ladies.

Perhaps all women have the ability to produce the look, and they just are unaware of its capabilities. Was it just the glasses, or could it be produced without their help? Maybe their mothers secretly train them when they are children.

"This will be of great help to you when you are older – just keep it a secret for now. You will know when it is necessary to use it" mothers might instruct their offspring.

However, in our house, things have progressed.

Spurred on by her initial success I have noticed a change in Val's body language.

Next comes the head slightly tilted on one side. This is "I hear what you say and consider it nonsense."

Then one leg will come forward and in the way that only women can, the hips are tilted. "I have considered it nonsense and now require you to attend to it" is the meaning here.

Now the hand will be rested on the hip with the straight leg. "You are not attending to it, and if you don't there will be consequences." To me, this is the red flag moment.

Finally, the free hand will rest on the nearest waist high point at wherever she is standing. I don't know what this means as I have never let it get this far, as it would be way too dangerous.

However, I think I have found a simple way to circumvent all this.

It's in the form of an emoji. I have carved these into my shortbread biscuits and I can now gauge situations perfectly by seeing which biscuit Val picks up with her coffee. Thus, the need for her to give me the look will bypassed.

Anyway Marge – I don't know if you are still around – but your legacy lives on.

...and as you will see – as a result, perfectly tasting shortbread, although the artistry ? Well, perhaps not so much.

Emoji Shortbread Biscuits – the ultimate test.

Time once again to visit the relatives after two years apart – this time on my own...

The Traveller *(July 2022)*

I was travelling up to Milton Keynes last week which involved taking the train from Euston. I left my case by the door and sat on the nearest seat.

Apart from the fact that the train was rammed with American tourists with hoards (and I mean hoards) of children, the reason for which I could not fathom, I watched as a variety of ne'er-do-wells boarded at the last minute.

I decided that my faith in human nature was such that I could see the case walking at one of the many stops *en route*. I think they call it stereotyping these days, but in my defence I saw them as stereotypes.

Anyway I moved the suitcase to the side of my seat and was working out if it was too large to fit on the rack above the seat, when I was interrupted.

"Excuse me sir" said a broad American drawl. "Couldn't help but notice – would you like some help in getting that on to the rack?"

He was mid 40's and seemed to be in charge of an inordinate number of offspring. His wife/partner/non-gender specific friend looked on appreciatively, as did a number of the children.

I was struck dumb. Was I looking that old? Were the wrinkles that had gradually crept up upon me over the years now displaying themselves in all their glory? Was the lighting system on board so designed that it picked out all the flaws in the more mature traveller?

I had travelled a long way today and the train was late so I might have been looking harassed at most. I was wearing T-shirt and jeans, looking, in my mind, no more than middle aged, but of course that was just in my mind. Maybe the reality was different. Maybe in America so many have had face jobs that they all look young, and he was not used to seeing a non-stretched pensioner.

"Err... no, thanks anyway but I'm fine" I responded.

This of course now meant that I had to be seen to put it on the rack with extreme ease. I contemplated trying to do it one handed, but thankfully thought better of it. That way, surely disaster was more than likely, and to make things worse they were still all watching me.

I picked it up, swung it up and round and it slotted (just) onto the rack. I hadn't worked out in all the confusion whether it fitted or not, but thankfully it did.

"What about a round of applause" I thought as I sat back down, and tried to look nonchalant. Happily they would never know that inside I was actually breathing a huge sigh of relief.

They all got off at Watford Junction, on their way to something called "The Harry Potter Experience" for which apparently there was a coach waiting. I couldn't work out whether it was the parents or the children that were more excited.

I on the other hand, travelling on, and observing my window reflection in the Tring tunnel, considered the wrinkles. Maybe he had a point, and watching the world going by at speed I came to the conclusion that it was about the same speed as my life was going by.

The Ferry and the Superyacht *(August 2022)*

We were on the St Mawes ferry.

This was on a day trip to Falmouth, so why take a ferry somewhere else?

Well, we saw that it was running and we took the George Mallory view, when he was asked why he wanted to climb Everest in the 1930's. (No, it wasn't Sir Edmund Hillary).

"Because it's there" he replied.

We got on it because it was there. Possibly not quite in the same league, and also what we didn't remember was, it didn't end well for Mallory so best perhaps to stop the analogy there.

Out in the bay we came across this superyacht, lying at anchor which caught the attention of every passenger on board. It was almost like a spaceship had landed in Carrick Roads and was now quietly waiting to wreak havoc on the town of Falmouth – although actually it was pointing at Truro. As long as it didn't turn and point towards St. Mawes, we weren't worried.

The Superyacht named "Pi"

We both speculated as to why it was there.

"I reckon it belongs to a Russian oligarch and they are hiding it away from the British authorities, safe from sequestration as no Civil Servant in Whitehall has heard of Cornwall much less having been here" was my take on it.

Val considered this.

"I think that now all the fast food chains have left Russia, it's the nearest place they could go to for a Mcdonalds" she replied.

"Actually, I've just looked it up" she continued.

"It's called the "Pi" and it is worth £120m. It takes 125,000 litres of fuel."

"Got it!" I exclaimed "That's why they are here. Diesel is only 182.7p at Asda Falmouth...I mean, who wouldn't."

I did the maths.

"That's only £228,375 for a tankful. How shrewd – no wonder they are billionaires!"

I had done 'artisan' with my emoji shortbread so I considered it high time I went upmarket. Oysters. They used to be a staple of the 'working classes' until they were over-farmed and the prices started to rise putting them out of reach of most of the population. Now they are glamorous, sophisticated and stylish.

Oysters *(August 2022)*

"I think I should up my game with my cooking." I had decided that I wanted to try something a little more sophisticated with my next venture.

"Well what did you have in mind?" queried Val, suspiciously.

"Oysters! I'm going to have a go at oysters."

Oddly she was not displaying the amount of enthusiasm that I thought was commensurate with my announcement. After considering this proposal, she came up with a suggestion.

"We could just go down to the bay and drink seawater" which wasn't really the response I was expecting.

To be fair I could see where she was coming from. I had experimented by purchasing one from Morrisons a while ago in order to test out what all the fuss was about.

It tasted exactly of that. Seawater! Actually slightly slimy seawater.

I put it down to my artisan upbringing that I didn't appreciate them. I don't remember having oysters at any time during my childhood. Mind you we lived in Catford, so perhaps enough said.

"No – these are going to be battered, beer battered or tempura..ed" (sorry – tried to turn that into a verb). "Anyway – I haven't decided which, but they clearly will need some texture."

I know nothing about oysters whatsoever, so it was research time. I couldn't see anywhere in the local supermarkets where I could buy fresh oysters so I went on line and found a site called 'Simply Oysters'.

Then an unexpected dilemma: Pacific (Rock), Kumamoto or Native oysters?

'Pacific oysters are nonspecific filter feeders, which means they ingest any particulate matter in the water column. This presents major issues for virus management of open-water shellfish farms, as shellfish like the Pacific oyster have been found to contain norovirus strains which can be harmful to humans', said the blurb.

Hmm... not sure you are selling your product too well there, 'Simply Oysters'.

They apparently harvest them from all round the country, but here's the thing – they had a number of Cornish locations but were all sold out. There were plenty available from beds in the East of England. I suppose the inference is that the nearer the Atlantic they were, the cleaner the water. Well, I bet they didn't know about the amount of sewage discharges from SW Water occurring on a regular basis.

Native oysters are only available to eat in the winter months when the water is cooler and the oysters are meatier. It's these oysters where the 'r' in the month saying comes from. The Kumamoto variety are small and sweet and farmed at Maldon in Essex.

So now to recipes!

As I was going for glamour, sophistication and style, I looked for the recipe which appeared to contain all those three elements.

By far and away the most glamorous, sophisticated and stylish sounding name I could find was that for "Rocky Mountain Oysters." I thought that if I was going to do this then I should go for broke and despite it being American and therefore having suspicions that it might not actually be as sophisticated as I wanted, I would go with it. Puzzling was that the title seemed contradictory – I couldn't see the marine connection here.

Also puzzling was the first paragraph – which word for word said "Anything that walks, swims, crawls, or flies can be eaten. It just takes an open mind and a willing stomach. Of course, there are some people who will eat anything."

"It's only oysters" I thought. Strange.

Ingredients listed were beer, eggs, flour, cornmeal, salt, pepper, vegetable oil and...

I can't even write it – it made me wince so much. (You will need to look it up yourselves). Suffice it to say – there were no oysters involved. "Sometimes they are pounded flat" went on the recipe, which actually made my eyes water thinking about it.

Surely never in the history of cooking could anything be more mis-named! You see, give the Americans independence and that's the sort of thing they come up with.

Val considered the recipe.

"Probably best if you stuck to a simple British version. One that actually includes oysters?"

"I was trying to be glamorous, sophisticated and stylish" I replied haughtily. Suddenly, in context, Pacific oysters seemed not so bad after all.

"I think if your previous cooking exploits are anything to go by, best stick to simple don't you think?" said Val.

Well I thought that my cooking skills were definitely on the up.

I decided to do simple but complicated! Simple recipe which actually included oysters but instead of choosing which way to cook them I would try the three ways.

"One dozen oysters, four with tempura, four with beer batter and four with ordinary batter." I worked my way through the necessary ingredients, all of which we had – except for the oysters.

Duly ordered from the same fisherman at Chapel Porth who supplied us with the lobster, to be collected on Thursday next and cooked for dinner.

Val has put it in the diary. "Oysterday."

Given my track record I thought she was being a trifle optimistic.

Oysterday *(August 2022)*

Well the day started with a downer. Our fisherman at Chapel Porth left a message to say that he could not get any oysters.

"OK" I thought. "Plan B then." The slight problem was that I didn't have one.

The last resort was a phone call to Waitrose at Truro. They exude glamour, sophistication and style of course, but you pay through the nose for it.

"We've sold most of them and we only have six or seven left" came the response... "and they can't be reserved."

We dived into the car, flew down to the store and arrived almost breathless at the fish counter. No oysters to be seen.

"That's no problem, I have a dozen in the back" said the assistant. There was no correlation between what was said on the 'phone and reality.

"We'll take the lot" I replied, trying to be as blasé as possible. I've always wanted to say that in Waitrose.

I don't think that however *au fait* you are with oysters you would call them handsome. They look like bits of rock in their shells and a pool of slime when shelled. According to the counter assistant they are alive at the point of sale but you wouldn't know it – as a result in my imagination they just lay there looking up at me. I came to the conclusion that only another oyster could love an oyster.

I also made the mistake of researching them on Wikipedia – my advice is don't! There was nothing you could read there that would possibly make you want to eat them. However I was too far into this experiment to back out now.

You are supposed to shuck oysters and there is a special tool to use with a detailed description of how to do it on YouTube.

Stage one complete

I certainly wasn't going to buy a special tool, and at that point Val intervened.

"Don't you go using any of my best kitchen knives" she said emphatically.

"As if I would" I said, silently changing my mind. Instead I attacked them with a couple of screwdrivers and scraped them out with an ordinary knife.

"Is that glamour, sophistication and style then?" asked Val who of course already knew the answer.

"Look, it's effective" I grumbled in response and ended up with a bowl full of innards.

Val examined this. "You know what I am thinking?" she said.
"£13.50 and a trip to Truro – for that!" Looking at the 12 tiny blobs in the bowl myself, I could think of nothing to say.

I had three recipes for batter and worked through them in order and ended up with three bowls. First was ordinary batter, the second was with beer and the third was a tempura.

"You surely used carbonated water for the tempura didn't you?" quizzed Val.

"Not in the recipe" I said looking at the self named 'Bumblebee' recipe list. "But it does have paprika" I continued as brightly as possible. I don't think that helped.

"Interesting" she replied very slowly. I didn't know what she meant by that, but I had a good idea.

"Don't worry – it'll all be glamorous, sophisticated and.... Oh never mind." Even I gave up on that one.

The Three Mixes

Val was looking in the 'fridge at her one egg left. "...and how many of those did you use?"

"...er, five."

She looked at the oysters, then the batter, then the oysters again.

"Five" she repeated, and said no more. She didn't have to. There was enough batter to sink a battleship.

So now to 'batter up' and deep fry. I did this in stages and after four oysters in each bowl we tasted them in turn, giving them marks out of ten.

The Finished Article

Nice little side salad with them to make them the star of the show and away we went.

"Well – glamorous, sophisticated and stylish?" I queried.

She gave me one of her looks. I guessed not.

"Here's the thing" she replied. "That was a delicious, if small meal, and you can't argue with the way it looked but....all I tasted was the batter – I didn't get any oyster taste at all."

Truth be told – neither did I.

I sat there looking at three large bowls of left-over batter and pondering on the meaning of life, because at that point I knew my association with oysters was well and truly over as glamour, sophistication and style was definitely not for me.

As far as we were concerned life was completely back to normal ..and despite the world in general going to Hell in a handcart, some situations still made us laugh...

How to Catch a Train *(August 2022)*

Well I might as well admit it now – I love travelling on trains.

So as a birthday treat I wanted to travel on the new line they have just reopened between Exeter and Okehampton. Now we could have just driven to Okehampton and caught the train there but no – this was the real deal and I wanted to go from Newquay, which all told would take around four hours. See – it's all about the trains!

Which is why at around 9am we were sitting on the platform watching as a man, together with two women and three children disembarked from a large taxi together with more suitcases than people. This was interesting as it was only him unloading the cases doing around four trips to and from. The rest of the party were standing around doing, from what I could see, very little. Oh, yes...and he was holding a dog on a lead just to make it more difficult.

With the time rapidly approaching and with me really looking forward to the first part of the trip – the last thing I wanted to see was a yellow jacket with GWR on it on the platform because it is an unmanned station. That can never be good news.

The man sporting it was by now in earnest conversation with the suitcase party, and there looked to be a full and frank exchange of views taking place.

"Go on – find out what's going on" said Val with us both not liking the look of this.

"... and we've got to get to Heathrow to catch our flight" said Suitcase man.

"I'm sorry, but the train has broken down at Par so the service is cancelled" said Yellowjacket. "I've organised taxis to take you to Par – but they are not here yet."

There was now a crowd of about twenty passengers, all trying to catch the connection at Par, and before anything more could be said a minibus type taxi appeared from nowhere and parked right in front of us.

We did the honourable thing of course and got on it quickly just in case, along with six others and full up we were ready to depart, leaving Suitcaseman still remonstrating with Yellowjacket.

"There's more taxis coming" he said more in desperation than anything else.

He asked our driver to call base. *(This is word for word)*

"When are the rest coming" he pleaded.

"I find out" said Taxidriver in a heavy East European accent.

Taxidriver: "Contol ees anutter carr comin?" I think he said.

Contol (sorry Control): "Yes there are two more on their way."

Yellowjacket: "When?"

Taxidriver: "Contol, wen thay com?"

Control: "Yes two more."

Yellowjacket: "When? Half an hour? Five hours?"

Val: (whispering) "All getting a bit tense I think."

Taxidriver: "Contol, ow lon?"

Control: "Two more."

Now you would think that it would be the East European that would have difficulty with understanding questions but Control was totally British yet seemed to be on another planet.

"I didn't think that was a particularly hard question, did you?" whispered Val, who I strongly suspected was getting the giggles. Now was not the time to look at her as I thought it likely we would both crack.

Yellowjacket had had enough and snapped.

Yellowjacket: "OK get this one going" he suddenly said to Taxidriver, with everything else still unresolved. We departed with Suitcaseman still arguing his corner in the background.

"Actually I feel a bit guilty" I said to Val. "He's going abroad somewhere and we're only going to Okehampton..."

I thought a bit "...but then again, not that guilty" finishing the sentence.

You may remember the television programme "Mission Impossible" and the opening quote.

Well, we suspected that Taxidriver had received that message. "This is Control: Your mission, should you choose to accept it, is to... get them to Par in time for the 10.19." In the series, the message would now self-destruct. We wondered if that would happen to Control this time.

He had accepted it, and it appeared that nothing was going to stop him from succeeding. Music blaring and head down he catapulted us away... as far as Cliff Road where he screeched to a stop. Newquay traffic.

At this point Val decided it was enough of the music. It was "Every Breath You Take" The Police's stalker's anthem at the time. An indecipherable grunt followed as he unwillingly acceded to her request.

He also did not appear to like daylight, as he left absolutely none between him and the vehicle in front. This was at all times and if anyone in front got away his foot stamped on the accelerator instantly. As a result, he had to quite often stamp on the brake with equal ferocity as well. At that point we both now believed either we would get there in time – or die in the attempt – which was the bit that worried us.

"In Mission Impossible he usually succeeds" I said to Val reassuringly.

"I'm not reassured" replied Val reading my mind perfectly.

Now you might think you know the quickest way to Par. I thought I did. But there is a way that I think no-one else knows. This is to take the normal route but cut off all the bends, which had the added bonus of making for a very exciting ride. His piece-de-resistance was going to be the hill down from the clay pits to the Par road, with all the roundabouts. So far he had treated them as non-existent until the last minute, flinging us all to the right and then to the left. Val, in the middle hit me and the lady on the other side in turn as we spun.

"This could be adapted as the latest Alton Towers ride, it could totally outdo their Nemisis ride" I thought. I pondered on how it could happen but decided it could not be done because our ride was way too scary.

Never before have I been pleased to see a camper van in front of me which had appeared on the hill. This stifled Taximan's ambitions and seven passengers breathed a collective sigh of relief.

Flying into the car park at Par we undid our seat belts which was a mistake as for his encore he had to slam the anchors on to avoid a car coming out of a space and all of us ended up spreadeagled against the seats in front.

He beamed, as we staggered out, for him, mission accomplished, whereas for us, we were feeling more than a little seasick and also rather happy to still be alive. Control, hopefully not having self-destructed, would be pleased I guessed, and although nobody else in our group thanked him – Val did.

"Thank you for getting us here on time" she said sweetly, but he ignored her. I think he may have thought she was being sarcastic. To be honest – so did I! Finally, we crossed the footbridge and sat down to wait for the train.

Looking up I noticed a man ferrying suitcases over the footbridge going forwards and backwards, with a group of others standing looking at him. He had a dog.

Suddenly I realised. "Hey Val, look! It's Suitcaseman – he's made it." I was actually pleased for him, as he seemed to have such a hard life.

"There wasn't even a taxi there when we left" replied Val. "How on earth did they get here so quickly?"

It will be forever one of life's mysteries.

Our second holiday since lockdown. All thoughts of the virus assuaged, and in the end, despite Val catching Covid along the way, presumably because of all the injections, I never did.

The Holiday *(September 2022)*

Extraordinary!

Back home from our week away in the Isles of Scilly and I cannot imagine why Val is certain that I'm trying to kill her. As far as I can see the holiday was fine.

OK there was a slight problem when we had our five hole Isles of Scilly golf rematch. She did stand at a 45 degree angle as I took my shot on the 4th and I did manage to give it quite a bit of wellie.

It was just unfortunate that it took off at the same 45 degree angle, and headed straight for Val. She had no time to move but fortunately my rucksack was in the way and it embedded itself in it with an almighty thud, like some sort of cruise missile landing. I'm not good at golf. So in no way could I be accused of trying to take her out using a golf ball.

Fair enough, there was a small difficulty with the buggie we had hired for the day. I've never driven one before and I really was not used to it. I pulled out of a side road only to see a van approaching down the hill from the right. It was a left hand drive so Val was in the firing line.

It was just unfortunate that I wasn't quick enough to accelerate leaving us in the middle of the road. Fortunately, in the end I stamped on the pedal as hard as I could and disaster was just averted. So in no way could I be accused of trying to take her out by means of a road accident

Reasonable to say that I had a minute misunderstanding with what was wrapping up our butter. It was from a local dairy, and how was I to know that it was a foil based wrapper when I put it in the microwave to soften it, as it was straight out of the refrigerator.

It was just unfortunate that as a result the paper caught fire fuelled by the butter. The flames were quite extensive. I managed to extract it but it was still burning wildly as I put it on the worktop. I managed, finally to extinguish it. So in no way could I be accused of trying to take her out by setting fire to the holiday apartment.

Understandably I had not realised how difficult the coast path would be as we were walking around St. Mary's. There was no indication on the map that walking for someone who had a stick, so close to the edge would be dangerous.

It was just unfortunate that she became very frightened because of her balance problem, complaining loudly that if she fell she would almost certainly end up in the sea and she couldn't swim. I really did do my best to help her over the boulder strewn path. So in no way could I be accused of trying to take her out by deliberately taking her along a treacherous footpath.

I mean - how could any of that be interpreted as malign? I rest my case for the defence and I am off now to take out a nice big over 50's life policy on Val just to show her that everything is, as I said at the start, just fine.

Lockdown had provided me with the opportunity to learn to be a chef, and the story of my elevation to that of chef ends with the ultimate test. Was I on a par with the Two Michelin Star chef Heston Blumethal? Well I thought so, but for some unaccountable reason Val did not...

Experimental Cookery Part 1: Preparing the Ground *(October 2022)*

"Heston Blumethal."

Pouring over the newspaper on Saturday, I announced this across the kitchen, hoping to attract Val's attention as she also had her head buried in the supplement.

It had the desired effect.

"What about him?" she asked, I suspected feigning interest.

"Well, he's back" I said quoting from the newspaper. "It's made me realise that I want to move on from the everyday cookery I have been doing and start to attempt to tackle some of his two Michelin Star recipes, and as it happens there is one here."

"And what everyday cookery might that have been?" she queried.

"Does she want a list?" I thought.

"You know... for instance like the pasties I made, and the oysters... shall I go on?" I said.

"As I recall it averages out at roughly once every three weeks. It was the 'everyday' bit I was wondering about."

"Anyway, I want to get stuck into his recipes, they are really out there and it would be so interesting to do something totally original". I continued rapidly trying to get the subject back to firmer ground and to the matter in hand. "What do you think?"

She thought for a minute.

"Well, the last thing I read about him making was egg and bacon ice cream, and to be honest I think that is barking! I mean, why would anybody at all want to eat such a concoction?"

Now this is where I thought things were getting a bit tricky.

"In the newspaper, it has some of his simpler recipes, and as I now consider myself pretty adept at most cookery challenges thanks to the two years of enforced training due to Covid, I'm really up for it." I tried to sound confident.

"I'm thinking about your past attempts, and all I can say is 'some recollections may vary'."

"Actually, I think that quote has already rather famously been used. Anyway, in the paper he has a recipe for..."

At this point I nearly lost all my confidence bearing in mind what Val had just said, but almost invisibly wincing came out with...

"...bacon and egg porridge."

She was silent for a moment, and then...

"Well what about lard and fish paste cakes or perhaps chocolate and taramasalata?"

"Yes, that's it" I replied. "That's the sort of thing he's famous for – unusual combinations."

"Really?" Now a pause, then...

"Would you be interested to know that those combinations are from Latitia Cropley in the comedy 'Vicar of Dibley', put together for their comedic value. It seems to me that bacon and egg porridge would have fitted in quite easily."

I sensed it was time to put my foot down.

"Heston Blumethal is a two star Michelin chef and there is no way that he would allow a recipe in the newspaper that didn't work." I was quite emphatic. "I'm going to make it."

"Is sounds quite disgusting to me and I'm not going to eat it. Never in my life have I ever seen a poached egg on top of porridge." Val was equally emphatic.

"Bit previous don't you think. Look when I've made it just have a tiny taste and we'll then see who's right. I'll fully admit it if is as bad as you think, as long as you admit it if it tastes OK."

She thought for a minute.

"Here's a challenge" she replied. "If you're so confident, if it tastes awful you still finish the plate. If it is tasty, I'll finish the plate."

"Ha. You are on!" The deal was done.

Heston and I vs. Val. There should be no problem at all.

But on thinking about it I can't help but wonder if I have fallen for the 'Heads I win, Tails you lose' trick.

Experimental Cookery Part 2: The Chef's Table *(November 2022)*

There seemed to be congestion in the kitchen.

"Actually, what are you doing?" I asked as Val seemed to be taking over all the space I would require for my gastronomic delight/horrendous concoction depending on the point of view.

The Ingredients

"It's a fallback position" replied Val. "I mean, if I just rely on this bowl of ..." She tailed off for a minute.

"...I'm going to end up starving this evening. It's a sort of insurance policy. I'm making a caramelised onion and tomato with thyme tart."

"I'm also making two chicken and leek pies – I mean, I'm not saying that I have no confidence in your cooking endeavour, I'm just thinking it. You know you will be thanking me for this later."

"So that's two insurance policies then!" I grumbled.

"Can you draw out a couple of chickens in pastry and put them on the tarts." She was certainly rubbing it in!

Job done and all out of the way, Val back in the other room watching a film, it was time to get started.

As usual, the first job was to pour out the wine. Nothing to do with the recipe – I just always drink it whilst cooking. As before I refer to Graham Kerr, Keith Floyd for those of a certain age, and I'm sure other well known chefs partake so I am in good company.

I dealt with the prep. and even in saying that I felt quite the chef. All laid out in bowls following Heston's recipe to the absolute letter I was ready to cook.

Halfway!

To be honest, there was nothing to report. Everything that could go right, did.

So bacon, onions, mushrooms, stock, curry powder and Greek yoghurt all chucked in to the mix at various times finally adding the oats. What I ended up with was basically yellow porridge.

So on to a tray and presented to Val with her egg on the side as requested.

Voila!

She tasted it.

A long pause and then the verdict.

"I really don't believe this. It cannot be right. It can't work – and yet..." Another of her pauses.

"It really does work!"

She ate the lot – as did I.

I will admit it now – I had lost confidence in the whole project but having started I could not back out as I felt I was on some sort of impossible to stop conveyor belt, heading for oblivion.

"It's incredible how things can change so quickly" I thought.

We sat silently for a while with the film burbling away in the background whilst both of us knew there was an extremely large elephant in the room.

After I while I made a comment.

"If it's alright with you I think I will give the tart and the pies a miss tonight" I said with an air of total innocence.

I said no more.

A few Post Scripts here – Life has gone on since Cronavirus but now a new set of problems regarding the economy were now making life a bit more difficult. But we soldier on...

Economy *(November 2022)*

"22 pence." I said it loudly so that Val would take notice. Given all the economic gloom that was flying around at the moment, I thought we should play our part in economising.

I had just filled the car with petrol and noted the mileage. I worked out that we were running it at 22 pence per mile.

"So to go to Truro it would cost getting on for £5. Then there is the car parking. Well for that sort of figure we ought to be going on the bus – which is free!"

"So what are you saying?" said Val knowing of course we were going there today to do Christmas shopping, returning an item and then for her to do whatever she does when she goes shopping on her own – I'm not sure what it is but it always seems to take hours.

"We're going on the bus" I announced grandly. "It doesn't take much longer than in the car and it practically takes us door to door. Think of the money it will save, and don't forget the carbon footprint."

Actually after the important stuff was done I spent most of the rest of the morning in the M & S cafe with a latte and a newspaper whilst Val then did whatever she does when she goes shopping on her own.

On the bus back she was silent for a few minutes and then...

"Are you in tonight?" she asked with an air of total innocence which I always find worrying.

"I'm going to the Par Track actually. We've a training session there, and I'm taking the car as I'm giving someone a lift."

She paused as if thinking things through.

"So, because of the cost, we don't take the car to Truro to do important things like Christmas presents and returning stuff, but we do take it to Par when all you do there is run round in circles?"

"That is just not the case" I replied "Not right at all." I deliberately sounded incredulous.

"Sorry, but I don't see how it isn't right" she replied.

"Well – Par Track is an oval."

A Book Dealing Story *(November 2022)*

Our usual Sunday today, and after I was out on a run this morning with one of my sons, Val and I Sunday lunched at the Smugglers Den, and whilst not being particularly enamoured with the background music in general they suddenly came out with the Rolling Stones' "Satisfaction."

"Strange choice" I thought.

However, being of what they now call "a certain age" we started to reminisce. Not for the sixties, given the music playing, but our life after my retirement from the Building Society world, and of our life as bookdealers. A Rolling Stones story sprang to mind.

We were always available for house clearances and we had a call from a lady on the Roseland to clear a small library, as she and her husband were leaving London and moving down to Cornwall to live in their holiday home, so they now needed the space. Well, that made a change from death, which was the usual reason we were called in for clearances.

We priced our offer, and as I was chatting to her I noticed volumes of photograph albums on one of the walls. I asked if I could look and discovered that there were a large number containing many photographs of the Rolling Stones in their early days.

"These are pretty good, don't you think" I said as I discussed them with Val. We didn't make an offer as it was outside our comfort zone but I remember saying to the lady "Wouldn't it be great if you had the copyright, they would be worth a fortune" and we all laughed.

We had only recently been to the Hall for Cornwall and had seen the Counterfeit Stones, which was a really great evening.

"Look, seeing as you and your husband are really into the Stones why don't you go and see them – we really do recommend their gigs – a great night out." I was on a roll.

"I thought they were fantastic and I wasn't a fan of the Stones at all when I was young" added Val.

"Furthermore, at the price the Stones themselves charge for a gig, it is way too expensive. I mean, come on, why would you pay that sort of money for a seat, where, even if you are lucky, you'll see them as specks in the distance." I was really banging the drum now.

"The Counterfeit Stones are so much better value for money. Make a note next time they are down – really I promise you won't be disappointed." I added hoping to convince her.

"Good to know" she said, in what I thought was a rather non-committal manner.

The subject seemed closed, so we did the deal, loaded up the books and went on our way.

"Happy with that?" I asked Val.

"Yes, a good deal I think" she replied.

Val thought for a minute.

"Those photographs though. I'm sure they don't realise what they've got there. I hope we gave her an idea of what they could be worth. It's a pity that we are not in that business."

"I'd loved to have done a deal on those" I agreed. "Still we are OK on the books."

I don't know why, but after pondering on the call for some time, and for no reason at all that I could think of, I put the husband's name into Google.

I really couldn't believe it.

"Val" I shouted.

She came rushing in.

"What's the problem?"

"No problem as such..." I replied.

"...only that was the wife of one of the the Rolling Stones official photographers and we've just told her that they are not worth seeing and that the Counterfeit Stones were better."

"We really are true professionals" giggled Val.

(Later research showed that prints of his photographs sell for £500 each and upwards)

What is SMS? *(November 2022)*

I'm beginning to feel my age.

We were sitting watching 'The Great British Bake Off' last night (OK that makes us old in itself, fair enough) or rather Val was watching it. I was just staring vacantly at the wall. I find I can do that quite easily these days, and to be honest I quite enjoy it. But that's not the event that sparked all this.

The telephone rang – not the mobile but the land line (yes we still have one). Nobody rings us on the land line any more. First thing it did was stop me staring at the wall and instead I started to stare at the phone.

"Who on earth could that be?" I queried.

"There is a way of finding out" quipped Val as I answered.

A mechanical voice bellowed out (it was on speaker) "This is an SMS text message."

This is where I realised that once again this age thing was gradually enveloping me in its cold insidious tentacles.

"Never heard of that, don't know what it is and if I never get another one I guess I won't be that worried." was my only thought.

But it continued.

"from..." and there followed a number I didn't recognise...

"Crystal Palace are playing on Amazon Prime now."

"To listen to the message again..." I hung up as there was now a necessity to enter inter-sofa negotiations with the Bake Off contingent.

To be fair Val has always said that we could watch the Eagles play any time they were on television. She is on safe ground of course because it happens usually only at maximum a couple of times a season. Bake Off put on record, and there it was, the match about half an hour in. Now I have a pretty poor record when watching teams play live.

As an example, in 1993 happening to be up country visiting relatives, I had an afternoon off so I went to see Wycombe Wanderers play. They had just been promoted to the Football League for the first time in their history and were smashing all before them. Never having been beaten at home in the league I saw them play Colchester United. They lost 2 – 5.

With a record like mine I should have known what would happen. In under 30 seconds after I turned the match on, Wolves scored. I wondered if I should send an apologetic e-mail to the club.

"With a record like yours you should have known what would happen." said Val looking up from her book, for some unaccountable reason not watching the match.

However, sticking with it, for once things went my way, and we won 2 – 1. So all in all a good evening.

I have still no idea what an SMS text is, who or what sent it and how it knew I was an Eagles fan, but thanks for the message – even if it was from a 'bot'. I've certainly changed my mind about receiving them and am looking forward to the next one.

Should be some time next season.

The Near Death Experience *(November 2022)*

I was out with a group foraging under the expert tutelage of a seasoned forager. We walked along the footpath from the car park at Crantock to Penpol Creek and back looking for various plants to sample.

He would stop by a particular plant, and pull off some leaves.

"Roll it round in your fingers and crush it." Which we did.

"Now sniff it." Which we did.

"Now eat it." Which we did.

He would then bombard us with facts about each plant, so many actually that there was no way we would ever remember them all.

So he went through the same procedure with Sorrel, Sea Radish, Oxalis, Rock Samphire and many more.

To be honest, whilst he was waxing lyrical about the different nuances of taste, all I could discern was that some were sweet, some salty and some peppery. That was about it. I'm such a peasant.

We got to Penpol Creek where he stopped at another plant by the stream and once again picked it and handed leaves round to us.

It looked particularly attractive so I decided to taste it straight away and was about to do so when he went on...

"This is Water Hemlock and is seriously deadly poisonous. I just wanted to show you that it was safe to handle, and so in future you will be able to recognise it I've just put on a bit of a show to emphasise that.

The Water Hemlock

I immediately dropped it, suddenly realising that he had not this time followed up with "now eat it."

"Hell's teeth, that was close" I muttered to myself quickly trying to be as blasé as I could be and showing everybody that of course I never had any intention of eating it.

I looked around. The path was strewn with Water Hemlock leaves and everybody else was also being blasé, and trying to look as if they never had any intention of eating it.

Now I don't know what serial killers look like. I guess nobody does, because if they did, they'd all be locked away by now. Might this be the next one though? I decided to take note of all his distinguishing features so that I could spot him should I be called to an identity parade at some stage in the future. It did also occur to me at the same time that I might not make it that far.

I decided to carry on with the walk, but from then on to be very, very careful.

He cooked up quinoa at Crantock beach at the end of the walk. He added the proceeds of the day to the mix and we all were given a plateful.

...although as I was eating it I couldn't help but notice that he hadn't taken a plate for himself.

Saturday Mornings *(December 2022)*

Saturdays have a certain ritualistic quality about them these days.

I get to the kitchen first and prepare everything for breakfast, go and get the newspaper from the local shop and we sit down to a meal of croissants, orange juice, tea and coffee. We discuss the various important topics from the paper in detail over breakfast, putting the world to rights so to speak.

This morning the important topic was – what was the silliest title of a hit pop record either of us could think of, and which one of us could come up with the best example.

Well, we are of a certain age and therefore can go back to the 50s with names.

"OK" said Val. "What about 'Itsy Bitsy Teenie Weenie Yellow Polka Dot Bikini'?

"Not bad." I countered with "'Mama Weer All Crazee Now' by Slade?"

"No – that can't count, they deliberately spelled things wrongly. They did it for effect ...and anyway I can come back with 'Do Wah Diddy Diddy Dum Diddy Do." she replied.

Hmm... that was a good one.

"Wasn't it just called 'Do Wah Diddy Diddy' though?" I pondered.

"'Dum Diddy Do' really needs to follow on, don't you think? Well it would if I had written it." Val was quite emphatic.

"Not sure that this conversation is going anywhere" I said.

"You think?" giggled Val.

"Actually, I've got 'Does Your Chewing Gum Lose Its Flavour on the Bedpost Overnight?' That was by Lonnie Donegan – and I had that in my collection, a number three in 1959."

"You really are older than I thought" she opined.

"Right! Then what about 'Um, Um, Um, Um, Um.' Wayne Fontana, 1964 or was it 65?" I was on a roll now. "Those were the times when you had to ask for a record title in the shop. Imagine asking for that now. The assistant would think you are barking."

I think we both considered it a draw as breakfast continued in silence for a minute probably because we had run out of both titles and enthusiasm for the subject.

The pause was interrupted by Val.

"Don't tell me you bought that as well?" she sighed.

"Not saying," I replied.

The Tale of the Three Refrigerators or "A Fridge Too Far" *(December 2022)*

We only have an undercounter fridge in our house, which usually is ample for our needs, as there are only the two of us now.

Some time ago a friend was getting rid of their fridge and rather than dump it, as it was still working, they offered it to us. Val thought that we could store it in the garage and use it when various members of our rather large family were due to visit. It seemed ideal.

A few days ago I got the call...

"Ray, can you switch on the fridge in the garage? Because we are entertaining on both Christmas Day and Boxing Day we really do need it, as there is a large food order coming on Tuesday" said Val.

It had not been on for six months and I had this feeling that things might not go too well. This feeling of melancholy deepened as I noted that the interior light did not switch on.

Left it a couple of hours and... nothing.

"Sorry, but it's not working." I came back after rechecking and confirming in my mind that I had been right – things were not going too well.

I have always found over the years that Val can solve most of the household problems very efficiently and quickly. This was one of those occasions. She considered the position and came up with the solution...

"You just need fix it by Tuesday afternoon when the delivery is due."

See – problem solved.

It was me that now had the problem – how to fix the fridge.

"Check the fuse, and see if there are any wires that have come loose" was helpful advice from Val, all of which I did, and adding one to her list. I kicked it. I wasn't sure if it was to help or just out of malice but I enjoyed doing it anyway.

"Well something has to happen. I've got all this food coming and nowhere to store it. You have to think of something."

Even the fates were conspiring against me. A really long cold snap meant that there was no need for a fridge anyway, but it was due to end big-time just before the delivery.

I bowed to the enivitable and shelled out to buy a new fridge online, and for an extra £20, I could have it delivered on Monday. This was on Friday. I'm way too mean to pay that so I decided I'd go for the click and collect option and nip into Truro on Monday to pick it up.

I received an e-mail to say that they were working on my order and would let me know very shortly when it was ready. Nothing received on Friday and halfway through Saturday I contacted them as Val by now was climbing up the wall with worry with no e-mail being received.

"We're here to help" said the blurb on their website, followed by "Reach Out" (Don't you just hate modern sales jargon).

I reached out, on the left, the telephone was to hand and on the right, the web page open at the same time. Immediately on the right a little webchat box opened in the corner of the screen, whilst on the left a large number of options had to be chosen on the telephone – after which I got the music.

On the right I clicked on the box. "Hi. My name is Deepak. How may I help you today" came the typewritten reply.

I basically asked "Where's my fridge" only slightly more politely.

"It is being delivered by DPD to the local store, but we are sorry, there is a delay" came the response.

"If I paid the extra £20 they said I could have it on Monday, so they must have it" I quoted from the website.

"It is being delivered by DPD to the local store, but we are sorry, there is a delay" came the response again.

"How long might that be?" I asked.

"It is being delivered by DPD to the local store, but we are sorry, there is a delay."

I don't know why it took me so long to realise Deepak was not a person, but I finally clicked. I cancelled the web chat and immdiately got a message – "How did we do?" I gave them my answer.

Meanwhile on the left hand side the music was still playing, interrupted every few minutes by a friendly voice informing me that they were experiencing an exceptionally large number of calls at the moment but would be with me as soon as possible.

I have this theory that one day a business will say "Your call is not important as it is not a sale so we have put insufficient staff on this line. They are all on the sales lines. That is why you will wait a very long time for us to answer." As a result they would surely succeed because of their refreshing honesty.

Eventually I gave up.

"I'm just going to go down to the store on Monday and sort it out with them direct" I said. "It seems to be the only way."

Monday came.

"I've had another sleepless night, I've got all this food being delivered tomorrow with most of it needing to be in the fridge, and still nowhere to put it. I'm going to get on to them myself." Val, in panic mode, made the call.

She got the options, of which there were many, then the music...but eventually – success. An answer, this time a real person.

"It is being delivered by DPD to the local store, but we are sorry, there is a delay" came the response. The telephone was on speaker.

"You aren't related to someone called Deepak are you?" I muttered.

"No – this time definitely a real person" whispered Val with her hand over the telephone.

I've mentioned before about Val's ability to assume "The Look." The glasses slip down the nose and she glares over the top of them, and I am convinced she could defrost the contents of the freezer with it. She was now glaring at the telephone. Would it work down a telephone line? Would it teleport? Would the Deepak soundalike be traumatised and decide that this job was not for him after all?

We would never know, but whatever the outcome she was immediately passed to another department and to someone who started to sound somewhat sympathetic.

"I'm not sure what the problem is because they have plenty of that model in stock at Truro. I don't see why they can't just let you have one of those and just keep the one being delivered" was the extremely logical assessment of the way forward.

"Neither can we" sighed Val. "Look, I don't care about anything anymore, I just want a fridge for Christmas" she pleaded. She had gone from concern, to worry, then on to impatience and now to desparation.

It was agreed that we go down to the store and if there was no joy we would just purchase another one there and then, and cancel the previous order.

At the store we explained the problem to the assistant. We put forward the suggestion.

"Oh no, that can't be done" he said. We can't let you have one of ours – different departments you see."

I didn't see and was just about to give up and just buy another one when a very managerial lady appeared and took control. After yet again explaining the problem, she said "Before we do anything else – let's just check to see if it was in fact delivered."

Five minutes later she reappeared.

"Yes – it's in the warehouse, just go round the back and pick it up."

Now I know I should have taken them to task about no-one bothering to check and let us know, but I was too far gone now, we just did exactly that, flew back home, and it was installed in the garage that very afternoon.

Rarely has Val looked quite so happy.

After stocking up the fridge on Tuesday and all now sorted she came back into the house.

"You'll never guess. Whilst I was there I just checked the old fridge." She paused.

"It's working now."

Someone who knows about such things advised us later that in very cold conditions, refrigerators can develop faults if the outside temperature falls below that of the desired fridge temperature for any length of time. It was likely that this was the cause of the problem.

Never Volunteer *(January 2023)*

There is an old saying... "never volunteer." This is reputed to be an old army expression, whilst in the Air Force or the Royal Navy it is expanded to "never volunteer for anything."

Well, I've never been in any of the services but I have discovered that this is equally true at home. Val, years ago once mentioned that she had to mash some potatoes... and I volunteered. Since that time, I have always had to mash the potatoes, and I guess that it is now my job for life. Lesson learned you would have thought!

But sadly not so.

Val was making a fish pie with a crusty pastry top.

"You know what would look good" she said. "There is pastry left over and we could just cut out a little fish and add it to the top."

"I'll do it" I volunteered. Ten seconds cutting it out, a few lines on the fin and it looked just the part.

What was I thinking?

The next time she suggested that I should do two fish swimming in opposite direstions, having taken it for granted that I would be cutting one out anyway.

Worse was to come. It was on to a beef and ale pie and I was asked to cut out a cow. I got a picture off Google and copied it out.

Val made a chicken and leek pie.

"Oh good." I thought I could get away with a leek, but not so.

"No, I really do need a chicken. Who puts a picture of a leek on a pie" came the response

I now had to master that art of drawing a chicken.

So today I came in to the kichen to be presented with a game pie, a pastry board, rolling pin and a pile of pastry. I had the suspicion that Val always deliberately keeps enough pastry behind in order for me to produce something for the top.

"It's got duck, pheasant..."

I stopped her there. "I'll do a duck then" I asserted firmly. I thought trying to cut out anything else would be even more difficult. A duck is basically round with a few bits added on I thought, forgetting that I'd have to cut out webbed feet.

"Actually I need two ducks as I'm splitting it in half for two meals."

"Thanks a bunch" I thought.

"No problem at all" I said.

So I searched the internet for a reasonable picture of the correct size, printed it off, then cut round the edges to use it as a template, flattened the pastry to the correct thickness and cut round it. I was so long getting round its feet that it occurred to me that it took longer to do that than it did to make the pie. Then the same again of course. I did think on looking at the result I could enter it for the Turner Prize as I considered it quite artistic (well, apart from the feet).

So there we are. I realise that still on the cards are sheep and pigs, and I am wondering whether I could get out of it if I turned vegetarian. Actually that is highly unlikely I think, as I guess Val would then be asking me to draw out a cauliflower, broccoli or some other root vegetable.

No, there is no way out of this one, and way too late I have discovered the risks involved in volunteering.

However at least I know now to stick with the forces approach in the future.

Ready for the oven – complete with Ducks

Well, we've come through it all now, and although Covid pops it's head out of the woodwork occasionally still, life is moving on and we now have a new set of challenges to overcome.

This diary has recorded some of the more memorable times over that period during which Val found a new favourite expression as a result. "What were you thinking!"

(David Atherton)

… and I have to say, looking back, I think I have to agree with her, for most of the time – what was I thinking?

The End